HOW TO BE HAPPY IN LIFE AND LOVE

A guide to living the life you deserve

Pascale Lane

Helping women to live confident and happy lives by understanding their past, realising how it affects their present and making positive steps for a brighter future.

Dear Juliane,

May you be Happy
in Life & Love
    Always!
It has been a pleasure
Working with you!
    Love Pascale

DEDICATION

This book is dedicated to my husband and children, without whom, this would not have been possible. For his unquestionable love and support of me through all my years of learning and development, I will always be grateful. To Amélie and Jasmine, who not only made me a Mummy but make me a better person and for whom I pray will grow up to be Happy in Life and Love always. I adore you and everything I do, is for you.

To my dear friend Amanda who has been a confidant, business coach, mentor, role model and counsellor to me throughout all of life's up and downs, I will always be eternally grateful to you.

To my Mum and Dad who have always believed in me and been proud of me and though the path has not always been easy, have taught me to believe in myself and have pride in my achievements.

To all my friends and family who have encouraged me, supported me, praised me and had faith in me, no matter what. You may not realise it but you have kept me going and I am grateful to you all.

And to the most wonderful Peter, who amongst being one of the most complimentary people I know, edited my book, with all its punctuation errors and still thanked me for the pleasure.

CONTENTS

INTRODUCTION

They say, everyone has a book in them - some people probably have a few.

This is my first book. I have waited years to write it. I've always had some great ideas but I've never had the confidence to do it. And that, I suppose, is the best place for this book to start. Confidence. Self-esteem. Understanding yourself well enough to put yourself out there and make the life you want for yourself.

How many of you have settled either in life or in love? My hunch, judging by the women and couples I have worked with over the last few years, is that a lot of women settle because they don't feel ready or worthy of taking the leap. They feel like they have to wait until the children are older, or until they have more time, they need more qualifications, they just need to lose a stone or two. Sound familiar?

I know it because I have been there too. During my years as a social worker, both unqualified and qualified, there were so many opportunities I missed because I didn't feel confident enough to go for them. I spent most of my twenties working two jobs because I had dreams and aspirations which I was desperate to meet but deep down felt I would never achieve because I just wasn't worthy of them. I wanted BIG but I was totally constrained by not feeling like I was good enough to achieve it.

The irony is that when I look back, I was the one who was always working, always studying, always trying to better myself in some way. It was only when I reached my 30s and I was married and settling down that I finally began to contemplate that I might be 'enough' as I am. Something shifted in me during that period of my life. It got deep and it got dark for a while. Through so much joy there was also incredible pain (I'll cover that throughout the course of the book).

The point is that only then, once I realised that I was worthy of going after my dream big-style, did the magic begin to happen. Once I started to believe in myself and understand my worth and know for myself without shrugging it off from other people, that is when things started to shift.

This book is a culmination of all my knowledge and all of my experience, both professional and personal, over the last 40 years.

This book is written to help you understand that you can be a slave to your past or you can use it to build yourself a bloody awesome life.

This book is written so that you can get unstuck from the humdrum life you feel you need to remain committed to, for whatever reason and go out there and make the change.

This book is written for all the ladies who want to be Happy in Life and Love.

This book is written for you, and I hope that you enjoy it x

1. HOW DID I END UP HERE?

So where are you now? What has brought you to this point where you feel change is needed? I guess that we all reach a point in our lives where we feel that we need something to change. Something significant. That could be to do with our relationships, either marital, friendships or even family (because let's not pretend everyone's family is the Brady Bunch!). Recognising the need for change in our relationships is hugely important. Some relationships remain because of habit, some because of loyalty and some remain because of blood. There are also relationships that continue because we don't see that the relationship is harmful to us, that it is toxic, clouding or dulling our vision and our glow. I will go into this in more detail in the Tribe and Influencers chapter later on.

Or maybe its not about a relationship. Maybe it's about a work or a lifestyle situation. Whatever it is doesn't so much matter. The point is that we all get to a time in our life, usually but not always around our 40s, where we take a look at ourselves and our lives and wonder 'is this it? Is this what I've been waiting or working my whole life for?' And that for some, can be a tough pill to swallow.

When we were children it's likely that most of us had an idea of what our life was going to look like when we 'grew up'. We may have had an idea about what career we were going to have or where we were going to live, whether or not we were going to get married and how many children we were going to have.

And then the shit gets real. We finish college, we might go straight to work, or go to uni, maybe travel for a bit if we're lucky, and then the bills arrive and responsibility comes in. Some of you may have had children young, got married young, suffered loss or trauma, and then before you know it you're in your 30s and you're on the hamster wheel of life. And around and around it goes.

Don't get me wrong, there's loads of fun along the way - just enough to mask or balance some decisions that you've made that have created a life path for you that you either didn't anticipate or plan to be a long term decision.

Let's not make this all doom and gloom. That's not what this book is about. This is not a heavy read about living an awful life full of tears and regret but it is about realising that for some (or many) women, life doesn't turn out how you thought it would. It curveballs, veers off, changes course and you're living your life, and it's a good life, and there are ups and downs the same as everyone else and you look around at your friends and peers, and they are living similar lives with similar ups and downs, laughing or crying into their latte or Chardonnay, and you think to yourself 'Well, I'm just the same as everyone else. We're all going through the same stuff, so I guess this is normal, this is just how it is'.

As a counsellor and coach, I have worked with many women who have come to realise that they are settling, either in life or love. They have created a world around themselves that is fulfilling everyone else's needs but often fails to fulfil their own.

I definitely had this moment when I was in my mid 30s. I was married and just had my first child. I had to return to work after five months which absolutely broke my heart, but we were scraping the money together to pay our mortgage and bills and I had accrued a lot of debt from a business venture which had massively failed. I wasn't resentful of having to return to work so soon; it was the reality of mine and so many other working mother's lives.

My husband and I had been together for about 5 or 6 years at this time and though I loved him dearly, and still do, there were several times when I questioned what the hell was going on.

He is incredibly attractive (to me), can be very funny, charismatic and is incredibly intelligent.

He was also (and still is) totally in his own bubble, suffers with significant anxiety, and is most definitely somewhere on the autistic spectrum. When I first met Dave I was already working around Asperger's in my role as a family support worker and I immediately saw the traits in him. In the early years of our relationship we explored this together as around the same time his life/business coach had also queried it. Dave and I did a ton of reading, joined a support group and went to meetings and seminars. We never felt the need to get a proper diagnosis because at that point we didn't feel it would benefit him or us in any way. The early years of our relationship were, at times, incredibly hard. When you love someone with all of your heart and yet feel invisible to them in so many ways, its heart-crushing.

When I was training to be a counsellor, I was still working and had just had our second little bundle of chaos, Jasmine. I would study on a Saturday and return at 6pm to find the house not only completely turned upside down but the breakfast and lunch still all strewn around the kitchen and dining area. It felt as if all he could manage to do was keep the children alive. And then he'd say to me 'What's for dinner?'

If I'd had the energy to do it I would have booted him out several times. My hormones were all over the place, I was working as a social worker, studying to be a counsellor, responsible for all the childcare arrangements and the domestic household stuff. Very rarely did he cook me a meal or do anything that would have either been helpful at the time or demonstrated love for me.

I was at one of my lowest points. I couldn't conceive how I could carry on living my life like this. I didn't want it to be like this but I didn't know how I could change it either. I didn't want to be a single parent but I also didn't want to be in a marriage where I felt invisible and utterly taken for granted. I needed something to change but I didn't know what.

But something was changing in me. Something really significant had recently shifted in me and that slow change pretty much altered our family's trajectory completely. I had started reading a book called The Secret while I was in Ibiza, 5 months pregnant with Jasmine. This book categorically changed my life forever. Later on I will go into more detail about the Law of Attraction and the power of intention and mindset but for now I am going to leave it as a notable game changer in my life.

Significantly what I learnt is that what we concentrate on we invite more of. If we are consumed by negativity we continue to be surrounded by negativity. It's everywhere we turn, in everyone we meet, in every aspect of our lives.

However if we concentrate our heart and mind on positivity, love, patience, forgiveness and gratitude, guess what happens? We see all of those things in everything we see and touch. Literally, mind-blown!

So instead of concentrating on all the negatives I chose to focus on all the positives. I had been into a dark place in my mind several times before throughout my teens and adult life which had taken me down paths of either legal or illegal self-medication. Some of it was fun for a while, but the longer-term effects were not. I also used Prozac at a couple of points to manage mood swings and uncontrollable PMS.

In reality, there was only one thing that I loved more than my husband and that was the family we had created: two little girls who were, and always will be, my absolute world. I was certain I loved Dave and I knew deep down we would never have separated but the need to create the best world that I could for my children was *the* most important thing in the world for me. That's what it was all about. That was the reason for the struggle and the hardship, the studying, the change in career: it was so I could build a life around them, for them.

I began to identify all of the positives in my life. I wanted to be able to clearly see all the benefits that he brought into my life, both in terms of his personality, the errands and jobs he would do for me and the gifts he would buy me, but more significantly for me, the freedom I had to be myself; to grow and develop, to see my friends and go away if I wanted. No question, no quibble, just total assurance. Whenever I have wanted to start a new course or develop a new skill, he never questioned it. Never asked how it would fit around him. He would accept that this was part of my development and he would help me find a way to make it work. Whenever I wanted to go out for a day or a night or away for a weekend he never questioned it. We just had to make sure he wasn't working and the children were OK and that was that, no question.

Dave and I have always had unconditional love for each other. No question.

But most of us need more than that. Knowing that someone will love you and stand by you always, no matter what, is a wonderful and precious thing. Something that is actually quite rare, I think. But for some women (and I talk about women because that's who this book is aimed at although I 100% acknowledge that everything in this book can be flipped for the men) it's just not enough.

We need more than just love. We need independence, friendship from our partner and our friends, commitment, ability to grow and develop, respect, self-respect, opportunities to travel or to have freedom, not be taken for granted. Emotional, Physical and Spiritual Well-being!

And so that was the start of my journey. It wasn't until I started to work with women, both individually and as part of couples work, that I realised there were so many women who, for whatever reason, were living their lives with their glass half full. In fact, part of the reason why I moved from counselling to coaching was because my work often became so much more animated when I was able to share strategies and ideas with my clients and generally be more creative in helping women to live the lives they really truly deserved, to help them acknowledge that they didn't have to live a mediocre life and that there were ways that they could create the life for themselves that they truly wanted.

Now let me clear one thing up straight away before I go any further, because this is really important. This is not a man bashing book! This is not a book where I encourage or promote women going out there alone and ditching their husband because life is so much better alone! Absolutely not!

With my work I have met many women, most of whom have found a way, through the skills and advice I have shared, to either commit further to their married/family life or, for those who have recently separated, to find the confidence to create the new life they've been longing for.

I remain happily married, with the usual bumps along the way that all marriages face, but I have also created a life for myself that in many respects runs parallel to my husband. Does that suit everyone? No, absolutely not. Do I think it should? It's totally up to you and what works best for you and your family.

You can take whatever you want out of this book.

Whether or not you can get one golden nugget or ten, all I am hoping to do is to let you know that there are ways of living a fulfilled life that don't require you to take drastic action but to be honest with yourself, understand your blocks and self-limiting beliefs and then create a vision of what you want to achieve.

That's all it is. That is what I hope you will learn over the course of this book: to be able to identify what you want to change, to acknowledge the bits that work, the bits that need more work or support and the bits that need to go.

Being self-reflective is no mean feat. It takes courage, but it also takes something else. It requires you to be able to sit and be really honest with yourself. Honest about the person you are, understanding your strengths and flaws and, crucially, understanding how you got to where you are now. What was your role in landing in the position or place that you are now in.

This doesn't mean being hard on yourself and

giving yourself an emotional internal beating. This is just about looking back on your journey, understanding what or who were the main influencers in your life, who or what changed your path. What effect did that have on you? How did you respond? Know and acknowledge all of the steps that got you to here because once you know that journey and you can see what the rewards were along the way, what the hurdles were you had to overcome, how those experiences informed you getting to this very point in your life, then and only then can you begin to move forward, consciously creating the life you want. Whether the changes you need are big or small is irrelevant. This is about you. How you feel in yourself. You having the knowledge and confidence to tell yourself what you want and need in order to be able to go forward and get it.

Sarah was in her mid-40s when we started working together. She has three children aged between 10 and 23 and separated from her husband two years ago. However, even though separated for some time now Sarah was very much still under his emotional control. She is a highly educated accountant who although now running her own business after a career working in the family accountancy business, was very stuck. Not because she didn't know what she was doing or because she didn't have the insight or knowledge to manage a business. It wasn't even because she was a busy working single mother. She was stuck because throughout the 20 years of her marriage she had completely lost her confidence. She had lost the ability to see herself as good enough and able to run her own business. She knew what she needed to do but she was up against a wall which although totally self-built, was stopping her from moving any further forward. Her lack of confidence came from her marriage and the years of emotional abuse that she had unwittingly suffered. She didn't realise this was the case when we started working together but soon into our work began to describe stories and incidents whereby she had been completely invisible in her marriage, when, for instance, he would not speak to her for often weeks and even months. She became so worn down by this behaviour, being made to feel insignificant, invisible, not worthy of any interaction whatsoever on his part despite the fact that she was a loyal, loving, intelligent and genuine lady who was doing a marvellous job of raising their children, running a home and working in the family business. Sarah had got so used to this behaviour she naturally started to assume that the problem was her. She would often be the one to apologise, beg for forgiveness, hate herself, question herself, question everything about her life and her existence. Obviously, this had a huge bearing on the children who after some time also began to show signs of anxiety and depression. In retrospect this was very easy to understand, but still she blamed herself rather than the dismissive and uncaring behaviour of her husband, both within their marriage and towards their children. He was a very controlling man who withheld not only emotion but words and any kind of acknowledgement or affection too. Slowly throughout our work together Sarah began to understand his behaviour. Although he was still legally her husband he had not spoken to her since the separation three years before and refused to participate in any legal or divorce proceedings. Together we found her strength and her voice. She began to understand his behaviour and began to understand how she, *with all due respect to her, had allowed him to treat her like this and had colluded in his abusive behaviour. Of course she was not to blame in any way at all for this, but by allowing him to treat her like this she gave him the means to continue this behaviour for years and decades.*

Not only is she now insightful, stronger and more confident, she is also excelling in her business. The confidence that she regained in just a few weeks of working together meant that she was able to take her business to a whole new level: running workshops and helping fellow entrepreneurs, self-employed accountants just like herself, to have confidence in themselves and their businesses so that they can be like her, building a business that works around herself and her family.

She is a wonderful woman, a wonderful mother, a wonderful business owner and one day may well go on to be yet again a wonderful wife if she chooses to!

2. PAST EXPERIENCES: LOVE AND FAMILY

This Be The Verse

BY PHILIP LARKIN

They fuck you up, your mum and dad.

They may not mean to, but they do.

They fill you with the faults they had

And add some extra, just for you.

But they were fucked up in their turn

By fools in old-style hats and coats,

Who half the time were soppy-stern

And half at one another's throats.

Man hands on misery to man.

It deepens like a coastal shelf.

Get out as early as you can,

And don't have any kids yourself.

I do love this poem. I remember when my dad first recited it to me many years ago not knowing whether to laugh or cry.

Understanding where we come from and crucially, where our parents come from, is, I would suggest, essential when it comes to understanding ourselves and having a clear idea of what we want out of life and what is blocking us from achieving it.

I could literally write a whole book on just this subject and maybe one day I will.

Throughout all of my career I have been fascinated by the cycles and patterns that continue through the generations. Often we can consider these patterns to be negative but that isn't necessarily the point I am trying to make. I'm far more interested in how, from infancy, throughout childhood and into our adult lives we absorb behaviours, stories, characteristics, body language, flaws and positive traits from our parents, all without having the slightest clue that we are doing so. All of these family patterns (as well as genetic predispositions) with regular reinforcement cement these patterns into our psyche. Half the time, we are not remotely aware they are even 'things' let alone that they are our family things that we are more than likely going to pass onto our children and grandchildren to come.

Another thing that I learnt as a social worker many years ago is that even if you are aware of these 'things' (and let's say flaws for the sake of this point) you can try so desperately hard to do things differently, to not repeat those mistakes or behaviours again when what actually happens is that you just end up repeating them in a different way, not avoiding or circumventing them but actually just recreating them in your own unique way.

How crazy is that? I have seen families of alcoholics, perpetrators of violence, most commonly of all though, emotional abuse and neglectful parenting, often visit the very behaviours onto their children, despite being so very angry, disappointed or hurt that their parents had inflicted that onto them as children. Sadly, it is most likely that their parents had also done the same.

To be fair this is a pretty broad and sweeping statement. I'm not saying it to be shocking or cause offence, I'm just pointing out that very often these cycles of behaviour readily repeat themselves unless you have a very strong awareness and determination to work through the issues and change them.

When my husband and I were preparing for our wedding, we weren't attending church and didn't want to get married in a church because we felt we would be hypocrites if we did. No offence to anyone, this was a purely personal decision for us. We had both been Christened as children and were definitely curious but we weren't ready to have a full-on Christian wedding. We did however want our marriage to be blessed and so we approached a wonderful man called Reverend Peter and asked him if he would bless us at the end of the ceremony. He agreed but asked that in order for him to give it meaning and to know and understand us better, that we attend his 6 week Marriage Preparation course at his church.

We happily agreed to it and thought it would be quite interesting but not really the 'game-changer' it turned out to be.

The course wasn't heavily religious although it was certainly arranged by a large Christian organisation and so did have a fair amount of religion in there. What was more surprising for us both though was the exploration of our own families and what we would by default be bringing into our new family.

Now as I said at the top of this chapter, this isn't necessarily about positive or negative traits but more about the basic and fundamental 'rules' if you like, of what a family looks like. What roles do a wife or husband have? What role do the mother and father have? How do you decide about house chores, money, financial stability, work roles and (my husband's most memorable lessons in the whole course) whether or not there should be a bin in every room downstairs or just one in the kitchen, and who is responsible for emptying them. I have no idea why this resonated with him so much but he pulls this one out frequently when describing to others now to communicate and negotiate things and I genuinely have no idea why!

I suppose the thing is that most of the time we don't realise the patterns that follow us into our adult lives and relationships because we are too close. Most people don't sit and reflect on their childhood or family history and even if they did, wouldn't be able to be detached enough from it to be objective. You might be able to identify certain stories and patterns but the likelihood is that you only have a close-up view and can't really step back far enough to see the bigger picture. It's so incredibly interesting, it really is.

So here's the point. Once you are able to examine this in more detail and really get a better understanding of how your family history impacts you now, you are then able to be free from repeating those patterns and, if you feel you need to, do things differently.

Let me give you an example. My parents were both committed to their careers and worked very hard. My mum ran her own business, a very successful children's day nursery. She worked incredibly hard to build her business and reputation and was very successful at both. She was a single parent and was absolutely doing her best, no doubt about that. She worked from 08.00 to 19.00 Monday to Friday and most Saturday mornings too although I was with my dad at weekends. With all this and the admin as well by the time she had finished she was emotionally 'spent'.

When I hung up my social work hat to run my own business as a therapist and coach I did so with the sole purpose of spending time with my children.

I didn't want it to be the same for them as it had been for me. I wanted to be around every minute of their day when they weren't at school. Call me needy, I don't care. I basically wanted to be a full-time mummy and a successful entrepreneur all at the same time.

I worked as much as I could while they were at school but inevitably had to work a lot of evenings as the couples counselling work meant that one or both clients were working a day job and so needed evening sessions. When I was home with the girls, after school or in the evenings, I was glued to my phone posting on social media, creating marketing material, chatting with prospective clients, trying to get organised and build a thriving business.

When the girls had after school activities I would be on my phone, working. When we had school holidays, I wouldn't book in clients but I would sit in the park on my phone working. I would go to soft play with my laptop and be working.

It was only when I hired my own coach and did

some full-on intensive work with her, that I realised what I was doing. I had literally just recreated the same patterns again but just in a different way.

My heart broke, I cried so much. There was a lot of snot involved. But I was so grateful for that mirror to have been held up to me. You see, even I, at the time, didn't realise the importance of that lesson. I knew it wasn't how I wanted it to be. I knew there was no point giving up a day job to spend time with my children to then be working four nights a week, Saturdays and spend the rest of my time on the phone but I hadn't realised the importance in the parallel I was creating, the one that I had tried so incredibly hard not to repeat.

And that is the point I am trying to make. Not all of the habits we recreate are necessarily bad. There are all sort of patterns and behaviours that make up our lives that are absolutely fine. Many of you reading this may not see any issue with being a self-employed working parent. I was building a future for our family and technically I was with them. After all, we are all just doing our best, right?

However, this wasn't what I had wanted. It wasn't how I wanted 'my story' to be. I had tried so hard to create a different story but in fact had just repeated the old one with my own unique twist.

So ask this of yourself: what patterns are you repeating, good or bad? What traits or characteristics have you inherited from your parents that you are mimicking in your current relationships, either with your spouse or your children? We all do it so please don't think that you don't.

So many of the chapters in this book overlap. I am so excited to write this book because I feel, for now at least, that so much of it makes sense once you are able to see the bigger picture. So many of my clients are, in many respects, in the dark when it comes to a lot of their personality and behaviour and it's such a privilege to be able to accompany them on their journey of self-discovery and change.

OK, so then what?

Well this is going to be very individual because it

depends what your background was like and what you've picked up along the way. There may not be anything that's too difficult for you to deal with in which case just having an awareness of certain characteristics is enough. It can make such a huge difference just to know and be conscious of these things, then if you catch yourself doing or saying something in a certain way you can adjust or stop it if you need to, or else just smile knowing that it didn't start with you and it is unlikely to end with you.

But what if it's something more significant than that? What if this is a lifestyle that you have created for yourself or family that you were so certain you weren't going to repeat but lo and behold, there is it, as bold as brass.

Two things come to mind which can help greatly. First of all ask yourself if this can be managed by you yourself or do you need a neutral person to help you work through it? By this I mean a counsellor or a coach. If you think you need additional help choosing a counsellor or coach will make all the difference. Ideally pick someone who is both. This is just my personal opinion and I am not trying to belittle or dismiss any life coaches out there but as a trained counsellor and life coach I feel that the overwhelming majority of my coaching clients have stuff in their past that they need to unpack. Sometimes (though I concede not always) this requires very delicate and specialist support. My skills as a counsellor have been invaluable to me in my relationship and life coaching and I firmly believe that you can't build a successful and emotionally healthy future unless you are aware of and have worked through any past trauma or difficulty. This of course will be totally down to you to decide but I just ask you to be cautious and wary. There are no doubt many wonderful life coaches out there that aren't therapeutically trained but I feel there are plenty who are not skilled or qualified to deal with complex personal issues and could ultimately do considerable damage if not equipped to deal with some of the unexpected issues that invariably come up in a session.

The other option which, regardless of the above, I recommend everyone do without exception, is to start a journal. Now this doesn't have to be a 'dear diary' type of thing. I'm talking more about brain-dumping your thoughts and feelings onto a page. This is an extremely helpful way of being able to work through and process issues and works for everyone on every matter. It doesn't have to be a heavy emotional task, although you'd be surprised what comes out when you let your pen start wandering over the page.

This exercise serves to help you identify the issues, behaviours or barriers that you are carrying around with you and brings them to life so that you can manage them. Start by thinking about your current hurdles or blocks and then think about what the ideal outcome of that situation would be. Then think about everything (and I mean everything) that you associate with that and write it down. Have a big piece of paper and don't hold back. Think about your loved ones, partner, friends, parents, school teachers, bosses past and present, anyone you have heard a story or opinion from, and write it down. Think about your feelings during this exercise and what memories are coming up for you, too. The aim is to become aware of the stories you have embodied over the years and have become part of your norm. It need not be negative and traumatic. This could just be about patterns of behaviours that you have adopted that now serve to block you or hold you back in some way, or what you are telling yourself that is either self-limiting or dismissing, stopping you reaching your glorious potential. 'Oh I would love to do X but I'm no good at Y so that's that dream squashed' kind of thing.

Once you have done this exercise, keep writing. Not necessarily every day but whenever you think of something or realise something, write it down. Keep the journal active and write in it at least weekly. You'll be amazed how things start to link together and make sense once you have it written out in black and white. Journal keeping is an extremely effective therapeutic resource that is free and simple to use. You can use it as much or as little as you want but I do recommend everyone do it because none of us is immune to our past and all of us carry our family stories, fables and tales, to some degree or another.

Francesca is a lady in her late 40s. Her mother is Scottish and her father Ghanaian. She was born in the 60s in London Black people were largely discriminated against. Francesca grew up in a family of physical and emotional abuse. Her mother, a very hard lady, was both physically and emotionally abusive to all the children, and her father was the same. She would often recall how he would collect tree branches from the garden to come in and beat the children with. Although Francesca recalls many violent and aggressive beatings it was the emotional abuse which I believe did her the most damage.

As she got older she learned to channel her pain through poetry and creativity which she did very successfully and wonderfully. However, within her wonderful creative and gentle nature there was also quite a dark side. For a time she called this other personality Cynthia, the chimp. The naughty chimp. Cynthia would come out at times of stress and would be completely irrational and aggressive. Cynthia was fed on a diet of inner pain, unresolved childhood trauma and cocaine. The cocaine binges never helped and it was certainly a poison to Francesca, but once the cocaine habit stopped Cynthia didn't completely go away. She would appear at times of stress, anxiety and sleeplessness. She was most prominent at times of insecurity which were largely fuelled by mundane disagreements with her partner.

After a short amount of time we realised that Cynthia was not in fact a chimp but a little girl. Her name was also Francesca and she was a wonderful little girl who was desperate for love and affection. She craved her mother's love even though it was almost totally off-limits. In her older age Francesca's mother had become more or less housebound after several debilitating strokes and so the relationship between the pair changed significantly. Francesca began to understand certain things about her mother which she hadn't previously known, through having conversations about not only her own childhood but also her mother's earlier years. This gave Francesca context, which ultimately was a huge factor in beginning to heal her pain. She began to understand her mother in a completely different way and as a result of that began to understand her own childhood in a different way too. Don't get me wrong, the bruises very much remain, but she has learnt over time how to tend to those bruises and how to give them the love that they need to heal. Once Francesca was able to understand that young Francesca needed love and compassion she started meditating with young Francesca: sitting with her, talking to her, understanding her and healing her. Of course, little Francesca will never go away. She is a fundamental and essential part of history and present but understanding little Francesca better meant that big Francesca could understand herself better. Whenever feelings of insecurity arose in disagreements with her partner they were both able to acknowledge her and speak to her and give her what she needed in order to feel safe.

The impact of understanding this process was no short fix. Sometimes I would sit with Francesca and watch her sob her heart out. We would sit in silence and my heart would break a little bit. Sometimes I managed to hold back the tears and sometimes a few little escapees would trickle down my face, the pain in my chest burning like fire. But this pain was so powerful and so healing. She was able to release little Francesca in these moments and in doing so, in allowing herself to cry and release the pain, the changes in her were just immense.

I am so grateful to have been on this journey with both

Francesca and her partner, and give her what she needed to live a happy and fulfilled life. Of course there will be bumps along the road, no-one ever says there won't be and who would want a totally smooth path? Her future is now not only happier but filled with so much more understanding which she in turn will be able to pass on to those who need it.

3. TRIBES AND INFLUENCERS

How important are the people in our lives in making us the people that we are today? In all of the work that I do I always ask people to consider this. There is a massive difference between your Tribe and your Influencers but most people don't know the difference.

You may well be familiar with the concept that you are the average of the five people you spend the most amount of time with. Research has shown that this expands much wider than just your closest five and also includes their 5 people, social media, TV, literature, environment etc. The main concept to understand here is that we are all sponges and we all give and receive energy from each other. We absorb each other's energy, ideas, moods, aspirations, values, negativity like sponges. Because of that we all have to be very careful about who we are spending time with.

Often we think that we have little choice over the people we spend time with and so much of it is out of control. For example we might think that our family is our family and we are, for the most part stuck with them, be that a good or bad thing. The people that we work with are out of our control and we can't just choose who we share office space or shift patterns with. Whilst there is obviously some truth to these examples it slightly misses the point.

We must be aware who in our life brings us happiness and who doesn't. Not just that, who shares our goals and values? Who is the person that when you have an amazing idea, whatever it may be, you run to because you are so excited to share it with them? And who is the person you absolutely wouldn't share it with because you know hands-down they will either mock or ridicule you?

I make no secret of the fact that in terms of my tribe I am incredibly lucky in terms of love and business. My best friend of 20 years and my husband and partner of 13 years are both entrepreneurs. They have both grafted for the past 10 to 15 years and have learnt the system inside out. They have made their success through hard work, grit and determination. But not just that, they have suffered as a consequence. Relationships have been formed and lost. They have had ups but they have also had many downs.

In my time of local authority employment, middle pay-scale, annual leave, sick pay and pensions, I often wondered why the hell they did it. OK they had the privilege of being self-employed and working their own hours but equally they never stopped working. My husband took his laptop on our honeymoon and worked every day and my best friend works on every holiday she ever goes on, even though for a time she was lucky if she had one family holiday a year.

Yet now, several years on, they are so strong! They know their shit and they are good at it. They might not be millionaires but they have made it and as a result I have two champions who not only love me and believe in me but keep me propped up whenever I feel the need to collapse and curl-up in a heap. They can give me their advice (even though at times I have been overwhelmed by the tsunami of information) and together we are growing our empires.

You see, I have also believed in them the way they believe in me. I have been their number one fan throughout every step of their journey even though there have been many times in my marriage when I wished my husband would just get a regular job and be more available to me and our children, but that's not the point. The point is very simple, to make sure you hang around with people who believe in you, the ones who have got your back even if they can't visualise your goal. I'm not talking about 'yes-people'. No one wants or needs a yes-person in their life. I'm talking about people who believe in you and know that you will get to where you need to be because you are driven, determined, resilient and motivated. Fact!

When my best friend was having a wobble a few years ago, I said something which came out if my mouth before I'd processed what I was saying. She was worrying about money and was at the time spending way more than was coming in and I said very matter-of-factly "You'll be fine. I'm not worried for you at all, you'll be fine."

She looked at me shocked. 'You don't worry for me'? She asked. 'No I don't' I said, 'I definitely worry *about* you, but I don't worry *for* you. I worry that you might be unhappy, working too hard, being OK in yourself, but not *for* you. You'll be absolutely fine. You're amazing, driven, resilient… you're everything you need to be and you will be fine. You will smash it, I never have any doubt about that.'

That conversation has always stuck with us both. I

believe it about her and I believe it about my husband too. I've never doubted their ability. When we surround ourselves with people who believe in us something incredible happens. It's a bit like velocity. It takes on a life of it's own, gaining momentum and creating an energy which just exudes off us.

This can be, and will mostly be, the people in our lives. But it also includes what we expose ourselves to: social media, press, TV programmes, books etc. What newspaper do you read? Who do you follow on Facebook or Instagram? How do you feed your brain and your soul? These are so important too because everything we do has a consequence, no matter how big or small. Now it's not for me to tell you what you should watch or read but I know for a fact that the more I pump positive messages into my brain the better I feel. I'm not just talking about cheesy affirmations and motivational phrases and memes you see on Facebook, I'm talking the whole whack. I love personal development and I love listening to people who have similar spiritual and ethical goals and values. I cannot get enough of Denise Duffield-Thomas, Wayne Dyer, Jen Sincero, Gabby Bernstein. I literally want to soak it all up. Arguably, once you've read a couple of their books, is there anything 'new' they can teach you? No if I'm honest, not really. Does that stop me listening to every book, podcast, webinar, YouTube clip I can get hold of? No Way! Why? Because it's their message that I love. It's the positive vibe that I connect to. Can Wayne give the same message in 20 different ways? Yes! Does it get boring? No. Well not for me at least.

I am always open to hear new speakers and trailblazers and I will download a new book at any opportunity, but my 'go-to's' when it comes to needing the comfort of soul-food is a guarantee I rely on everyday. No joke. One hour of exercise every morning listening to one of them and preparing myself for the day.

The most important thing is to be aware of those

around you and create yourself a tribe. You can include whoever you want. It might be friends, loved ones, work colleagues, business networking groups (real life or online) as well as all of the other ways to feed your brain and soul. Hang out with people who make you happy. They might not always share your goals, but make sure that they believe in you and your ability to achieve them.

Conversely, we have energy vampires. In the same way that we are picking up positive energy and vibes from the good ones around us so too can we be picking up the negative.

We all have one person in our life who is an energy vampire and we know perfectly well that whenever we engage in a conversation or meeting with this person we can feel the life being sucked out of us on the spot. Horrible as that sounds its likely very true if you think about it. Often these people don't realise they are energy drainers. Some people just don't have much self-awareness when it comes to knowing how to communicate effectively with others. They may legitimately feel like the world is against them and that they simply have to offload their woes on to anyone who is prepared to listen to it because that in some way validates their sorrow or frustration.

It could be that they are someone who you love and care for very much but there is always a drama around them and whatever it is they are doing in their life there is always a soap opera story line near by. They just can't help it. Either way and for whatever reason they don't seem to comprehend that most of the time we are not actually interested in their drama or crisis. We may well care about them, or maybe not care for them at all, but nevertheless don't have any interest whatsoever in their new crisis or pity-plea.

I used to have a friend who I cared an awful lot for and genuinely had no ill feeling towards at all but often I would be on the phone to her for an hour and not once be asked how I was. Literally, I could have put the phone down (I often had it on loud speaker) and do the washing up or cleaning and she would have no idea. After a while I realised that I would have this sinking feeling in my tummy whenever the name came up on the phone display and I started to avoid the calls. Gradually the calls became fewer and fewer and the friendship slowly disappeared. Do I feel bad about it? Yes, I do, genuinely. I think about her often and what a terrible friend I have been to her and how much I let her down but that's what I needed to do to protect myself. When I was going through shit times in my life I needed to protect myself. It's not about saying that my drama is more important than yours but that I need to look after myself which means knowing and understanding who and what is good for me and who or what isn't.

Who makes you feel heavy or burdened when you think of them? Do they make you feel guilty, sad or angry? Are you reaching for the phone now because you haven't made contact in a week and you feel bad about that for some reason? Who makes you roll your eyes in frustration?

Be aware of these people because often we are unaware of the impact they are having on us and yet they have the ability to really bring us down.

And what about the ones that just outright want to rain on your parade, those who tell you you're a dreamer, you're never satisfied with what you've got, the people who are stuck in their own comfort zone and want to keep you there too? This is a really important consideration. Often these can be the people who are close to us and are triggered by our dreams for better things. They don't understand why we need 'more' and possibly don't think we are good enough to achieve it.

These are the ones who have the ability to make you feel 'icky'. You might feel a sense of embarrassment or shame when you share a snippet of your goals with them. They have you questioning yourself and wondering which way you'll sabotage yourself first because maybe they are right and they have a point.

Or it could just be folk who are down-right negative people and you have very little in common with but for whatever reason you are spending a lot of time with them and they are the total opposite of everything you stand for but you're stuck with them and just have to accept them for who they are and count down the hours or minutes you are with them. Maybe they have very disparate political or ethical views to you and you don't even want to have a conversation with them because everything that comes out of their mouth just destroys a part of your soul.. (ha ha.... I have a few in mind here!)

Beware of your influencers. These people are the ones who drip feed into your brain without you necessarily realising it. Their negativity seeps into the cracks of doubt or weakness you might have and it leaves you wondering about your own moral and ethical standing. They question your superpowers and everything that you are and stand for making it exhausting being around them because you can't just be your wonderful, fabulous self. You have to be slightly on-guard all of the time, never able to let yourself slump down in comfort and relax into your happy, joyful state, always aware that at any opportunity they can pour doubt into your mind.

Then there are the ones in-between. Those you share similar values with or principles, where you work in the same environment or you consider yourself to be on the same page but not necessarily friends. Work colleagues are interesting because if you are employed you will spend the majority of your time with them and yet not necessarily have anything in common. You might be fortunate to form some really good friendships or maybe have a couple of people who you are totally ambivalent to, or even just don't like.

Being aware of those around you is so incredibly important. Of everything I talk about in this book, and in all of the work that I do, being aware of your tribe and influencers is one of the most important lessons I can teach you.

Trust me when I say the people around you can either make or break you. I cannot express to you enough the difference it makes to me in my life to have people who I know support and champion me, and I don't mean just my husband and best friend.

I have always relied on my friends enormously throughout my life. I haven't always led a wholesome life, some of it has been pretty out there in terms of chaos and crazy, but all of my friends bring value to my life.

Since being with my husband things have not changed, apart from giving up the nasty chemicals which seemed fun at the time but were no longer conducive to my life with Dave.

However, being married to a man on the spectrum can be extremely lonely and leaves you feeling pretty unimportant at times. He doesn't mean it and I have learned not to take it personally, but it has in the past been soul-crushing but an afternoon with my friends, either over a cup of tea, playdate in the park with the kids or a glass or two of wine in the evening can make the world of difference to me.

It's not always about affirmation. Though it is nice to hear your friends believe in you it's not always what I need. Often I just need to be around 'my people' and feel safe in their company, knowing that our love and support for each other is unconditional. It's literally priceless.

4. HOW DO YOU SHOW UP?

Who are you? I mean the real you? How do you show up? Do you feel you're a different person when you're at home, with your friends or at work? Is it OK to have different personalities and if so which one is closest to the real you? I find this so interesting because often we do have different sides of our personalities that show up at different times. When I look back, particularly during my twenties I was so very different around my friends than I was at work or with my family.

Truth be known during my twenties I'm not sure if I knew who the real me was. I had a lot of internal conflict and often tried to be or do what made others happy, usually causing conflict or turbulence in other parts of my life; feeling a loyalty to some at the cost of trust or love to another.

Does this resonate with you? There are so many things to consider here. How do you think people see you? Do people see the 'real' you or do they see a façade? Which part of your personality do you allow people to see and which bits stay totally hidden? Do you have any characteristics that you keep in the shadows because if people saw this side of you they wouldn't like you or might judge you?

Often people can seem confident and out-going when really they are quite shy or depressed and others quiet and reserved in public or at work when at home or with their friends they are confident and sassy.

I have found that this is very much the case with women. I know there's a whole thing out there about men not being able to talk about their feelings because they want to be 'macho' and there's a whole wave of 'mental health matters' intervention which is absolutely right and essential and I make no light matter of that, but actually for women too I think there is something about feeling the need to 'suck it up' and get on with it as if our own needs are not as important as those of our family or our children. So many women these days are working mothers responsible for the overwhelming majority of the childcare, housework, and social activities. They may need to be caring for elderly parents, sorting out kids clubs or parties, either keeping the house tidy or sorting out the cleaner, sorting out the food shopping, as well as buying whatever else needs to be put in the cupboards. It's not that all men are useless, it's just that as women I think we just get on with it. Obviously this is quite a sweeping statement, I know that, but on the whole I would say this is the case for most women and certainly the ones in my personal and professional network.

There are two things going on here. Firstly,

usually, we hate asking for help. We feel like we either need to do it all to prove a point, to demonstrate that we are strong and capable or we feel as if our partners should know that we need help and should do it without being asked. After all, they know the drill. Food doesn't magically appear in the fridge and cupboards, nor does it cook itself. Or tidy up afterwards come to think of it. The kids don't get themselves up and dressed in the morning and they don't prepare their lunch or get themselves to school either… well maybe they do at some point but for a long time there they didn't.

And then we look around at our friends and their setup, and we look on social media and catch up in the playground or at work and we realise that a lot of people are in the same boat and so we just put up with it and settle.

We put on a brave face, carry on and the show continues. And it has to continue because if it didn't, then what? What happens if anything slips or god-forbid, we drop the ball.

It's interesting because on one hand, as women, we do talk very openly. Most of us are pretty in touch with our feelings and able to talk quite openly about what is both wonderful and crappy in our lives. And we can do that in a funny way or in a serious way. We can often recognise what we know doesn't feel right, but within that, and within our friendships and peer groups, often we just kind of accept that's how it is. And how honest are we? I mean, really? How often do you tell your best friends that you only took the job because your dad would never have accepted you following your dream job or career, or that you only married Bob because you didn't think anyone better would come along and you were desperate for a child, or that you really fancy Sally at the office but can't tell anyone you're gay because your whole world will fall apart if you did?

When you sit and you consider your true self, how many decisions do you make based on what you think other people will think of you? Are you living a life that is true to yourself or one, even in part, because it is either what is expected of you or because you don't want to disappoint or let someone down? What do you think would happen if you started to live a life that was authentic, being honest with yourself about what you wanted for you and how you not only wanted to be viewed by others but how you wanted to view yourself?

A really powerful question I often ask my clients is would you want this for your child? Often this might be regarding a partnership, an unhappy or abusive relationship. If your daughter was in this kind of relationship would you be happy for her or would you want more/better for her?

This also works with lifestyle choices. Would you want your child to be in a situation or career that wasn't right for them, for whatever reason? Would you want what was absolutely best for them in order for them to be living their best life possible or would you want them to do what was best by others?

OK, this is a bit loaded, I understand that. Life

isn't that straight forward, right? We have roles and responsibilities that we have to fulfil and it's not just about 'me'; there's a bigger picture going on here and I just need to make it through until: the kids are grown up, my income is more stable, my husband is less stressed, my mum's in better health... Well, yes and no. All of these things are, of course, important and some things take priority over others but *you* are important too! At what point did we decide that it had to be one way or the other, so black and white? Why can't you be happy and commit to the other things as well?

Not all decisions have to be life changing. Not all choices we make need to be game changers. Sometimes we can just set the intention of how we want it to be in the future and then start making incremental changes to effect the change we want. Does that make sense? So instead of being terrified about quitting your job, selling the house and opening a flower shop in Paris, you consider doing an evening course in floristry or start yoga and meditation lessons as a step towards your yoga retreat in Nepal or you start learning Spanish so that when you retire the language barrier isn't a block to achieving your dreams of relocating to the Costa del Sol. These small changes start to become aligned with your true self and then you can start being more comfortable with saying and being who you really want to be.

There's something else really important that happens when we show-up as our true selves, honest and authentic. We become more trustworthy. This is a crucial piece of the puzzle and is essential in being valued and respected by others. When we are true to ourselves we align ourselves with our values and purpose. Being clear what we believe in and how we want to be, rather than just be seen, by others and how we want to interact with them is, for most of us, really important.

Most people place trust at the top of the list of

things that they value most in a relationship – not just a love relationship but any kind. If you don't have trust then in my opinion you have nothing. How many times have you met a person and just had a funny feeling in your tummy, something you can't quite put your finger on? Often when this happens we get an intuitive sense that there is something untrustworthy about that person and that has a huge impact on how we proceed in that relationship.

As a social worker and as a therapist and coach being trustworthy is something which is fundamental. If I am not trusted by my clients then I cannot possibly be a good match for them. Who would want to employ a therapist or coach that they can't be totally open and honest with when a huge part of that work involves them being vulnerable, where they need to feel safe knowing that I am going to take care of them and hold their emotional space with them while they manage their way through the process?

In my personal life too I value all of my

relationships and a huge part of that is about knowing that I am trustworthy. This isn't about saying that I am perfect. Far from it. Who is? I have made many mistakes and I know my flaws but within that I am also able to acknowledge when things go wrong and make amends for them either by apologising or by taking necessary action.

How many times have you been in a situation where you know that you have handled a situation badly and you have addressed it head-on? How good does it feel to know that you have either corrected your mistake or found ways to make it better?

And what about when someone lies to you or is dishonest with you? It's horrible. It makes you feel totally taken for granted and disrespected. There are some people who really struggle to tell the truth, who really find it difficult to be honest. I have certain people in mind as I write this and I have often struggled with why they do it. I have considered that maybe it's because they don't want to upset or offend the person they are lying to, maybe because they want to keep certain parts of their life private, or maybe they start by saying something a little bit untrue and then it takes on a life of its own.

I have a friend who never really lies but always seems to want to conceal a bit of the truth. It drives me absolutely crazy. What are they trying to hide? This isn't even important. It totally doesn't matter, so just be honest. Then I have other people I know who just blatantly lie. And you know they're lying because they're dumb and they can't hide the fact that they are and I've seen them regularly lie to others, so I am under no illusion at all that they also lie to me.

When people do this, no matter how big or small the untruth, it goes a long way to explain who they are as a person. I think this is a really important point.

When you are dishonest to others, you are tainting a part of yourself. How can you be showing up in all of your wonderful glory if you can't be honest about the smallest and simplest detail?

The truth is, not everyone is going to like you. There may be parts of your personality that people just take an instant dislike to but those very parts that are received negatively by some will be loved and adored by others. When you are an honest person people can't help but respect that part of your personality. As I said, they may not like it but they can't not admire you in some way for it.

People might think that I am loud and brash. That's fine. I am definitely both of those things. But I pride myself on being honest. If you ask me for an opinion I will give you an honest answer. I might say it gently, in a way that won't break your heart or shatter your dreams, but I will find a way to be honest. Does everyone like me? Hell no! Does it matter to me? Well, yes, of course it does. I am human after all but it doesn't matter to me as much as it used to. I have done a shit-tonne of work on myself over the last few years and I am totally 100%

solid with who I am now. Some people may not like me but I have no control of that. I can however control how I show up and be the best person I can be, for myself and for my family, friends and clients. Why? Because as I said above, for all the reasons that some might not like me, others warm to me and love me for exactly the same reasons. If I am loud and brash and honest I use that as my unique selling point. That's why I have the success with my clients that I do. If you want to pay someone to be a passive coach or therapist and not give you much interaction, then I am not your lady. If you want a coach that doesn't swear and will not tell you anything about myself or my family, guess what: I'm not your lady. If you want to work with someone who wears their heart on their sleeve, tells you how it is, calls out your BS when you're kidding yourself and invites you to be a part of my world, even from a distance, then I'm your lady.

If you want a friend who will love you adoringly and a be a loyal friend no matter what, but call you a twat when you're being one and admit that they haven't got time to meet up at the moment because they're just trying their hardest to stay alive and be the best mummy they can be, and that aside from children and work nothing else actually matters at the moment, then, guess what. Yep, your guessed it. That's me!

If you are living a lie then how can you possibly be living your best life? Whether it's a job or a relationship or a deep-down wish or desire makes no difference: being honest with others starts with being honest with yourself. What is it you want? Who is it you want to be? How do you want to be seen by others? Does any of it really matter?

Fundamentally I believe your energy changes when you are living an honest life, and energy is what it is all about. Energy is what makes us, both in terms of our physical presence and our energetic presence. When I spoke earlier about meeting someone and just getting a gut-feeling that something is off with them, that's energy. When you are meeting with a friend and there is a bad vibe between you, that's energy. When you go for a job interview and something is off-key but you can't work out what, that's energy. When you walk into a building or you're looking for a new home, it's all about the energy. When our energy is right because our core values are being acknowledged and addressed, everything changes. Trust me on this. I go into this in a lot more detail in the next chapter, Law of Attraction and Self-Worth, but for now, know this: when you are living a life that is true to yourself, everything (and I mean everything) will start to fall into place.

5. COMMUNICATION

This is what I refer to as 'the big C'. In all of my client work, both with individual women and with couples, communication is the one thing that most people get wrong. We all have an idea about what communication is or should be and yet most of us (myself included) can be the first ones to trip over it.

So let's get down to basics. What is communication?

Communication is, of course, how we talk and listen. There are various forms of it. We can do it with our words, our tone, pitch and volume. We can demonstrate it with our body language, our eyes, arms, hands and posture. We all know that words have meaning. How those words are delivered is actually more important than the words themselves. If I write: 'OK, that's fine, don't worry' how many different ways can you interpret that sentence? Go on, try it now, its hilarious. What about 'What do you want?'

When it comes down to relationships, be that in love or any other kind, how we communicate can be the making or breaking of it. I can't tell you how many couples I have worked with where the miscommunication is not apparent and yet neither of them are able to understand the other's perspective because they simply aren't able to communicate their feelings or wishes properly. Communication isn't just about what we say but also what we hear. We can all hear things differently from time to time. That's OK. We are all human and sometimes we just get it wrong.

Most of the time miscommunication come from a place of strong emotion and that's why, in my opinion, most relationships break down. The emotions take over and all too often we are unable to speak the words we need to say or hear the words we need to hear.

I used to be a terrible communicator. I make no secret of that fact at all. I have always been articulate, loud (maybe considered brash by some), outspoken but well-meaning, but when it came to issues which triggered me, in terms of fear or anxiety, I would either clam up or start shouting. The first couple of years after meeting my husband was the most wonderful and excruciating period of my life in some respects. As a teenager and young adult I found conflict incredibly difficult; paralysing in fact. If ever I was angry or upset about something I simply was unable to vocalise it. Don't get me wrong, people would know I was angry or upset, but to speak the words necessary to resolve the issue was just impossible for me.

When I met Dave, he would often have absolutely no clue what was going on for me. A total polar opposite to me he needed everything to be completely spelt out to the letter in order to understand what was going on. I remember the days when I used to say 'It's fine!' at him and he used to say, 'is that an A fine, B fine or C fine?' It became a bit of a joke in the end and was probably one of the first and most crucial steps in helping me express my frustration, as simple as that sounds.

Some couples like to scream and shout, some go sulky, but often they just don't hear each other properly. You see, if we aren't clear about the reasons we are feeling what we are feeling we can't possibly express that to our loved ones. Miscommunication in any relationship can happen for so many different reasons. Sometimes its about anger and frustration but often it is about hurt and pain which may not be related to the person in question but could be related to issues from our past.

I once worked with a lady who was an absolutely gem of a human being. Really lovely and as fiery as they come. She missed her family back home so much and although settled happily in London understandably wanted the gap between both of her homes to be so much less than it was. She resented her partner's relationship with his family. Although she loved her in-laws and knew they were wonderful, kind and generous people, she couldn't help but often be angry towards her partner when he chose to spend time with them. On the surface it felt to her that he was choosing them over her. If she was being stubborn and refusing to go she would expect him to stay with her. He of course didn't and this would often be a real source of contention and arguments. The more they argued the more she dug her heels in and compounded the issue because he would back down.

We spent some time discussing the issue to uncover the reality which was that she simply missed her parents and family. It wasn't that she didn't love his family but simply that she was sad that he got to spend so much time with them when she could only see hers once or twice a year. Being able to shine a light on that situation felt ground-breaking at the time. She just hadn't allowed herself the space to think it through and because her emotions were so strong, she wasn't able to articulate and share them.

Whenever I start working with a new couple I am always curious to find out more about the family upbringing. Yes the counsellor in me is always interested in childhood issues, but it's so much more than that.

Understanding your experience growing up is the absolute foundation to all of the work that I do. It's not necessarily about unpicking childhood trauma, although certainly that comes up quite a bit in my work, but about understanding what we learn as children about love. How did our family function as a unit? How did we witness love? How did we receive love? How was it demonstrated? How were disagreements managed? How was conflict resolved? How do we understand, interpret and demonstrate love ourselves? I know I have combined love and communication here and that is my intention because only when we understand these concepts can we truly know our value and our worth.

How we communicate as adults will very likely be rooted in what we learned growing up. Not just what we did ourselves but more importantly, what we were shown by those around us. If you grew up in a house where conflict was rife; where shouting and aggression was the norm, it is very possible that you will manage conflict in the same way in your own adult relationships. Probably 8 out of 10 women I work with have expressed concern at their children's behaviour. The children will start exhibiting either anxiety or aggression if there is conflict between the parents. That isn't to say that all conflict is aggressive. If you have a parent (usually the mother, but not always) who is withdrawn, depressed or anxious, the children are likely to pick up on that too and can often start displaying similar traits.

This isn't about bashing or blaming. Lord knows we don't need to be doing that to each other and that's absolutely not what I am trying to do here. All I am saying is that it is crucial as adults to both understand where our communication style and behaviour comes from and in turn ensure that we do not continue that cycle by passing it on. As a social worker I learned that cycles of behaviour carry on through the generations unless we make a conscious effort to break the cycle.

So when we are thinking about our communication styles and how we relate to our partner or loved ones it is so important to consider what we learned growing up. Take time to consider this because this is such a huge factor in being able to break any cycles you don't want to keep for yourself or pass on to your children.

Ultimately, most people would probably agree

that the best method of communication is to be able to speak to each other respectfully, calmly, openly and honestly. We all know how we want to be spoken to but are we good at demonstrating that ourselves? It's not always easy to keep calm and rational if we are feeling deeply upset or angry about something. Equally, it is not nice to be treated badly, shouted at or ignored and frozen out.

One thing I always find fascinating and make a huge conscious effort to demonstrate to my own children is that what we are modelling is what they learn. Monkey see, monkey do.

As adults, whether we are parents, teachers or similar, we drum into our children that they need to be kind, considerate, open with their feelings, learn to resolve conflict fairly and amicably and never to be moody or stroppy. And yet so many adults that I know, professionally and personally, don't do this. It's such a double standard and although I am in absolutely no way judging it, I just think it is something that we need to be aware of. This isn't about shaming people. Lord knows I'm not one to hide my emotions when I'm feeling flared up. It's simply about having a reasonable awareness that these things go in cycles. What we see, we learn and what we show, we teach.

And there's also something really important here about respect and self-worth. How are we willing to be treated and communicated to? What level of respect do we command for ourselves and what value do we put on ourselves? Regardless of our relationship status, how we value ourselves will be a pretty good indicator for how we are willing to be spoken to in all areas of life; be that love, family, work or other. If we don't feel good about ourselves for whatever reason, we may allow ourselves to be spoken to negatively.

In contrast, if we go through life with a positive view of ourselves, confident, self-assured and able to stand up for ourselves, there's not going to be too many people that will challenge us. They may not like it, but they are less likely to want to cross the line. And so, if we have learned from our parents and family growing up that we can manage difficult conversations calmly and rationally, that our voices and opinions can be heard readily and without judgement, then we learn that we are valued, we have a voice and that we have a right to be heard.

Catherine came to me because she and her partner were always arguing. They had a very loud and volatile relationship. She was a wonderful lady; loud, charismatic and vibrant. She had watched her mother be a "doormat" in her relationship with her father and Catherine was so angry about this. She was angry that her father had been such an aggressive bully, shouting and putting his wife down all of the time, but also that her mother would never stand up to him and would always just get on with it, but not a victim of abuse. I never got the impression she was scared of her husband, but was just ambivalent, ignoring him and keeping quiet for an easy life.

Catherine couldn't comprehend this at all. She and her husband came to have couples counselling at her request. He didn't really want to come but did just to appease her and shut her up. They were both volatile and at times uncontainable. She was so angry with him and had no issue expressing it; he would often shout back too, but mostly just wanted a quiet life. He would often remove himself and go and sit in the garden and drink a beer. This would escalate her anger and frustration and the cycle would just continue. He wasn't in anyway intimidated by her and they were in many respects both as bad as each other.

When I asked her about her behaviour, she was very clear in her response. She didn't want to be a doormat. She had witnessed her mother being so verbally beaten down over the years she couldn't bear to be the same as her. They had a young daughter themselves and she wanted to teach her daughter that women are strong and shouldn't be taken for granted or taken advantage of.

Once we were in a safe enough space for me to 'hold the mirror up' to her behaviour, she was devastated. All of those years of trying so hard not to be the doormat and she had in fact become the instigator. She was her father and she never even realised it. What an incredible lesson she learnt at that *time. She had focussed so hard on trying to make it different for herself and her daughter that she had gone full circle and repeated the history in her own beautiful way. She was delighted to have been able to observe this pattern of behaviour and manage to turn it around with almost immediate effect. Of course they remain a couple with vibrant and colourful language, that is just their style, but the level of aggression is so much less now that she is able to understand where it comes from and crucially, where it stops.*

You see, that's the difficulty. Unless we are willing to see it, and to be accountable for it, we just won't see it. Sometimes you need to be honest and reflective in order to see the things you don't want to or are unable to see. You need to be in a place where you are able to identify the parts of your personality that you both like and don't like, the bits you want to keep hold of and the bits you need to get rid of.

Understanding our communication style is so important. Communication is always a two-way street. How we are with one person will likely be different to how we are with another. Maybe not drastically, but enough for that dynamic to be completely individual. No two relationships are ever the same. And how we are in any given relationship dictates how that relationship will unfold. How we are treated in that dynamic is how we respond, and so the cycle continues.

So bear that in mind when you consider how you wish to be treated now and in the future. Can you look back on any situations and understand why it was the way it was? Whether there was love or conflict, what it looked like and what form it took? Knowing and understanding that can help the way we change things for our future and our children's futures.

6. LAW OF ATTRACTION AND SELF-WORTH

No matter what your beliefs are no one can deny that we all have free-will and we all have the power to reach our potential if we choose to do so. When it comes to dreams and goals I don't believe this to be any different. Everyone has the ability to make their dreams a reality as long as they have the right mindset and they are dedicated to the outcome.

Let's break this down. Most people have heard about the Law of Attraction. You may think it's the best thing in the entire universe or you may think it's a load of bollocks. For anyone who is not familiar with it and has never heard of or read 'The Secret', any of Gabby Bernstein's books, Denise Duffield-Thomas, Jen Sincero, Wayne Dyer, to name only a few, this is the Law of Attraction in a nutshell.

Everyone and everything, with no exception, is made up of energy and because of that we are all connected to the universe and have the ability to manifest anything we want. The premise is that whatever you focus your attention on will become your reality, so if you focus on negative things you bring more negativity into your life and if you focus on positive things, you bring more joy and happiness into your life. Sounds pretty straightforward right? Well, there's absolute logic to this but there is also a caveat, so stay with me.

The Law of Attractions works by encouraging you to have a healthy and grateful mind and life. Not only are you encouraged to have clear goals and desires but you are also required to visualise, meditate, practice gratitude and affirmations and use a vision board and visual prompts. Essentially this is about having a healthy and decluttered mind which allows you to identify your dreams and goals and believe with all your heart that they will become your reality. The steps, in no particular order, are as follows: Write out your goals so your intentions are clear. You can have as many goals as you like but I personally think it's better to have one general goal to work towards that is manageable and in reach. So for example, I have several goals which I want to achieve but most of them are going to be achieved once I have reached a certain income level so even though they are all worthy of being on my vision board, my overarching goal is to achieve a certain amount of income easily and consistently. That is my priority goal. Next, use a vision board with visual representations of what you are working towards. This effectively is everything you want to achieve in your ideal 'life' goal. For me, as I said in my example, this is all achievable once I reach the desired income bracket, but it's not about the money but about lifestyle, having time freedom, creating a life for my family that is aligned to my dreams and values. My vision board reminds me of what I am working to achieve and why it is so important to me. Then begin the practice of daily affirmations that start with 'I Am' so that you bring your future goal into the present as if they are already here and you are living and realising them. This can include ways that you want to think and feel as well as what you want to achieve. For example, I am prosperous, I am debt free, I am happy, I am pain free. The Law of Attraction is about practising a mindset that assumes you have already manifested your dreams into reality, even if they haven't arrived to you yet. They will come to you when the time is right. Have faith and know that they are on their way. Another step is to be grateful for all that you have. When you practice gratitude you demonstrate thanks for everything in life that you have, including lessons which have been hard to work through at the time but have taught you invaluable lessons and skills and you invite more positive things into your life. When we acknowledge what we have that is precious, be it your home, your health, your family, any surprise windfall, whatever you can think of, you attract more into your life because you are showing appreciation to the universe for what you have. I liken this to saying thank you or giving a compliment to someone who is not expecting it. When you show thanks to someone for something they have done you make them feel happy. They are then more inclined to repeat the behaviour or task because they enjoyed being thanked for it. Everyone benefits. Next, meditation. Not my strongest point if I'm totally honest but one I work at every day to get better at. Learning to quiet your mind and really slow down so that you can tune in better to the universe and practice your gratitude and affirmations with a calm and peaceful mind and heart. Only then can we process our situation and hear the messages we need to hear in order for us to know what we need to do next. If we are always busy on the hamster wheel of life we may easily miss certain signals and opportunities that may serve to help us achieve our goals more timely or effectively.

Why it might not work.

I hope you're still with me and I haven't freaked you out or put you off with that. The Law of Attraction is something that I absolutely believe in but I do appreciate and acknowledge that it isn't everyone's cup of tea. As a Christian I have often prayed to God and the Universe at the same time and wondered which one I am betraying the most in the process. Many writers have had similar debates and will state that there is no right or wrong here, that whether you call it God, Divine Being, Universe, Source, The One (or any other name you recall) makes absolutely no difference at all. As long as you believe in your divine entity you can call it whatever you want. The 'magic' happens when you set your intention and live your life knowing with all certainty that it will happen.

And this in-part, is why it works. A self-fulfilling prophecy is a prediction that causes itself to be true due to the behaviour (including the act of predicting it) of the believer. So the actions that we take and the decisions we make all lead us to reaching our goal. Now don't get me wrong, this isn't about making a wish, writing it down, putting it under your pillow and then waiting for it to just happen all by itself, you have to do the work too. However, the whole point that I believe is crucial in this chapter is that anything is possible if you put your mind to it. Don't get me wrong, I'm never going to be a supermodel or an international pop star. I'm never going to make my fortune in that way, it's never going to happen. Why not? Because I have no desire to do so and I have even less belief that I would be able to do either so it will never ever happen. However, will I make my fortune by helping people to live their best life, unpack their blocks, build their confidence and love the life they have? Absolutely YES! Why? Because I'm really good at it. I believe it.

I believe in myself and I believe that this was what I was put here to do. It's why I am writing this book because someone, somewhere, is going to read it and its going to make enough difference to them to change their life. I am not a guru but I do believe that when we believe in ourselves we can make anything we want our reality.

Here's the catch. I have worked with dozens of women (and men) who deep down don't believe they are worthy of their goal. This is so tough and this is why I said in the earlier chapter that you sometimes need to be therapeutically minded in order to work with certain blocks or issues.

Do you believe you deserve what you are asking for? Deep down, when you are alone with only your thoughts for company, do you believe that a person like you is able to have your dream life or financial income? What might it mean to you to receive your dream? What voice comes into your head when you consider even for a second that there may be a way of you achieving it?

This is so important because often we can have a goal in mind and we can visualise and create amazing boards and practice our affirmations and gratitude and meditate like crazy and yet, even after all that effort, nothing happens. What is that about? It can be extremely frustrating, not to mention really demoralising. The thing is, if you don't believe in yourself and you don't feel that deep down you deserve your goal, then it simply can't be delivered to you.

The power of the mind, the power of intention and the power of the universe all need to be totally aligned. If there is any seed of doubt in your mind that you are not good enough to receive your one true love, your happy ever after, your financial goal or whatever it is you choose for yourself, then you simply won't get it.

Now granted, often with blocks, a lot of it is down to worrying about what other people will think of you. People worry that they will lose friends and loved ones if they start shouting 'I AM A

MILLIONAIRE' from the rooftops. They worry about how they might no longer fit-in with their family and friends or deep down worry that life will change too much if they become rich.

But equally, they may just feel that they are not good enough for it, not smart enough, not pretty enough, or just not nice enough. One bad teacher in your early school years can make all the difference to you feeling like you are smart enough. One loving but overly critical parent can damage your self-esteem and self-worth for years, let alone an abusive parent or ex-partner.

So your biggest enemy in these examples therefore is you. I don't say that lightly, but I do say it honestly. You need to really be able to understand what your inner voice is telling you about what you deserve and what you are worth. If this is evoking some strong feelings or reactions in you then it is very possible that you may need someone else to talk this through and help you to make sense of it.

The overwhelming majority of people will have

blocks to do with their goal setting and everyone has their own ceiling as to what they think they can achieve. Most of the time these ceilings are quite low.

Having a low ceiling isn't the end of the world. In many cases it can actually be really beneficial because the easier it is to achieve the quicker you will achieve it and then you just keep going, incrementally increasing the threshold as you go.

So I invite you to spend some time on this and really give it some deep thought. Later on in the book we will be looking at personal development and goals and this will include thinking about how you work out what you need, emotionally, spiritually, physically and practically. We'll also continue to look at blocks in more detail and what we tell ourselves to convince us that we are either OK where we are (which is totally fine if you are genuinely OK where you are) or why we are stuck and unable to move forward.

But right now I want to stay focussed on the

stories other people have told you, the stories or words that have had the biggest impact on you that you may not even be aware of. Think about what your experience was growing up. Was it a happy and joyful experience? Did your parents champion you in everything that you did? Were you loved, adored and doted on or was your experience quite different? Were you a child that was misunderstood? Was your home fractious and chaotic? What words did you hear around you, either towards you or about you?

Ironically, both ends of the spectrum can deliver strengths and weaknesses and there is of course an ocean of grey in-between which also has its own pros and cons. You see, even if you have been loved and adored as a child you may have an abundance of self-confidence but if everything has been handed to you on a plate then the idea of setting some goals for yourself that are out of your comfort zone, which require you to achieve on your own, may not actually sit that comfortably. I have known people in the past who on one hand have had life very easy but then when they hit an obstacle in their path collapse and can't move forward. This is because they haven't had the opportunity to build the necessary resilience needed to keep going no matter what.

Carol grew up in a loving, caring and wealthy family. She readily admits that growing up she wanted for nothing. Everything she wanted, she got. She didn't consider herself to be spoiled but did acknowledge she was privileged and that she had a lived a lovely life.

However, this was not everything it was cracked up to be. Carol had never really had to deal with disappointment and had never learned to build resilience. She had always done pretty well at school, studied hard and achieved good grades. She had floated through her school and university years pretty well and hadn't had many knocks.

So when it came to her first attempt at running her own business she was totally unprepared for the amount of knockback she encountered. She had what was, in theory, an excellent business model but running your own business is far more than just realising a great idea. There are so many factors that need to be considered, adapted and changed, plus the fact that launching a new business can feel relentless. The hours that go into not just considering every single angle and concept and the practical application but also the marketing and all of the back-office stuff which you may not have even *considered.*

Carol came to me completely crushed. Her love life was hitting hard times and she felt the pull between her work and personal life an overwhelming struggle. She had never encountered any kind of significant resistance in her life before and so she had never really built up any kind of resilience. She was so used to everything being easy that she didn't know what to do when she met blocks in the road.

She took this as a massive blow to her self-esteem and genuinely thought that she would have to give up on her dreams. She felt she had gone from fabulous to flawed in the blink of an eye.

Once we worked together and she was able to understand that everything that was happening to her was part of her journey, necessary in order to not just survive but actually thrive, she began to turn a corner. She started to learn the strategies she needed in order to overcome these hurdles and take each one as an opportunity to learn. Once we see obstacles as opportunities to grow and improve they are no longer insurmountable but become something which we become incredibly grateful for, because they teach us to up our game and flourish. Needless to say, Carol went on to fly high in her business, life and love.

On the flip slide, a child who has grown up in a more challenging household may on one hand have low self-esteem or low self worth because they have grown up either hearing that they are worthless or just feeling like it because of pre-occupied or un-nurturing parents but ironically this could also be in some ways advantageous if it means they have learnt resilience and are able as a result of that to just keep going no matter what. Often a lot of the real success stories are from those who have triumphed over their difficulties because their story has given them fuel to raise themselves up and create a life for themselves and their family that is so very different from what they had experienced themselves.

For the overwhelming majority there is a huge area in between those two extremes where most of us fall, neither wonderful nor awful but challenging in its own way. These are the ones that can often be more tricky to unpick because on the surface it doesn't feel like the whole world is against you but there are equally big challenges ahead, for whatever reason.

Self-limiting beliefs can come in a variety of different ways and are often extremely convincing and hard to unlearn. Take time to consider your self-worth and how you talk to yourself when you think you're not listening.

The biggest hurdle you will ever have to overcome when reaching your goals and dreams is the belief that you can't do it or don't deserve it. Once you have trodden those into the dirt the rest is just application and patience.

7. HOW DO YOU SPEND YOUR TIME?

How do you spend your time if you really think about it? What do you do with your days, weeks and months that bring joy and value to your life? Do you feel that your time is spent doing exactly what you want to be doing, looking after yourself and prioritising your emotional and physical needs over and above anyone else?

The answer is most probably a big fat NO. You may even be laughing as you read the words to yourself. And here's why. As women, we are brought up from a very young age to care for others and put their needs before our own. The debate between what is predisposed and what is learned will always fascinate me but ultimately I think most people agree that the nature/nurture debate is 50/50; half predetermined in our genes and the other half activated through the environment and experiences we are exposed to, growing up.

When it comes to being adult women most of us have assumed some sort of caring role, either for a husband/partner, children or parents. It is innate. I don't think anyone would deny that. Even of career women who have married and had children, the overwhelming majority will have to balance their career, returning to work, looking after the children, arranging and facilitating play dates and after-school clubs, the domestic chores such as tidying up, doing the laundry, shopping, cooking and putting the children to bed... oh and taking them to school the next day after getting them up, fed and dressed the following morning. It's exhausting, and most of us do that whilst maintaining a full or part time job.

This isn't a chapter on women's rights, female

empowerment or even man bashing but simply to highlight that for many women the caring role remains predominant, even when work and careers are also in the mix.

And for those who are either unmarried or childless, the struggle remains. How many women do you know that without having children in the home, still maintain most or all of the household chores for their husband or partner? It's weird because it seems to be some sort of unspoken rule. It's not that men are in any way incapable of doing these things but I suppose that's just how it has always been. Maybe we are one of the remaining generations where most of our mothers and certainly our grandmothers were homemakers and maybe it's just taking time to rewrite the script for who-does-what in the family home.

Either way, my guess is that most of you ladies reading this book now will be champions at filling your time, chasing your tail and not really having much of a clue as to what you would rather be doing if you had the time. I mean there may be some fantastic ideas about spa days and massages or reading a book and drinking a cup of tea that's hot or even just hitting the High Street without anyone else or time restrictions. Do you feel you have a good balance in your life between your family, work, friends, hobbies and self-care? If you do that is fantastic. My guess is that most would say not. I'm not sure if I am being sexist here because I genuinely have no idea how most men would respond. Obviously for every walk of life there are variables and I only talk about the average in terms of most of the women that I know personally or professionally, as clients or as colleagues. This may be particular to the kind of person I spend my time with or may be more general. I presume it's the latter but I won't be making this a research project and this book is, after all, a light hearted glimpse into my brain.

That said, everything here comes from experience and knowledge. As I have been writing this chapter I have stepped away to do some client work and couldn't help but chuckle to myself when my client started to talk about how her ex-husband still relies on her for everything financial. Though not actually divorced yet but separated for some time now, he still calls her and asks her to deal with certain situations which she does because she is so lovely (I'm working on her. These things take time!).

How would you like to spend your time? I'm not talking about goal setting yet which we will come onto in the next chapter, but more about whether or not you feel your day is consumed by the needs of other people or whether a few tweaks are necessary to make you feel more valued and fulfilled.

Like many I feel my life can at times be a bit of a roller coaster. In the main my work/life balance is pretty good. I work my hours around my family as much as I can although there are the odd evenings and Saturday mornings that I see clients, but I know that won't be forever. It's short term pain for a long-term gain. My working week is busy without a doubt but my non-working time is equally busy and both of these are good things. Very good. I like to be busy and I like to ensure that my time with the girls is spent well. Admittedly I do not spend enough time sitting on the sofa relaxing. If I am sitting down with the girls, to my own shame, I will be working in some way shape or form, either on my phone or laptop. As I said, short term pain for long-term gain. It won't be like this forever but for now I am trying to build a life for us all that we will love.

So what do you need to do more of in order to feel like you are enjoying your days, weeks and months? What are the hobbies or tasks that you wish you could do more of or make headway in starting that would ultimately bring more satisfaction or pleasure into your life? Who do you need to be spending more time with? Your partner, friends, parents, book club? Why do you feel you are unable to get it done and what benefits would it bring for you to do it; and I don't mean the immediate benefit but the knock-on effect to the habits or people around you?

And what would you like to do less of? What are the things that fill your time that are either thankless or meaningless, that you could either just stop doing or delegate to someone else?

If you genuinely feel like you spend a lot of your week either chasing your tail or generally being less effective than you would like to be, I have two exercises which you may want to consider doing, either individually or together.

The first task is to keep a time log for a minimum of a week but preferably two. This doesn't have to be overly complicated but can be an incredibly effective way of showing you what you are doing with your time and how, if at all, you can improve it.

For any of you who have kept a food diary or a time management diary for your boss at work, this is pretty much the same thing. You literally log every single thing that you do from the minute you wake up until the time you go to bed, including how much time you spend in bed and what you do when you're in it! No joke, the full shebang. This way any ideas or (more likely) misconceptions about how much or how little time we spend doing something can be seen in actual terms. You don't need to show anyone this, it is totally for your eyes only so you can be as honest with yourself as necessary. Once you have completed this for a week or two, you can then write it out or make a graph or pie chart, whatever you prefer, in order to see quite plainly what changes you need to make. I personally love this exercise because in my experience, most women get this wrong. They overestimate some things and grossly underestimate others. It makes us more accountable for our time and leads us, if we want, neatly onto exercise 2.

Draw out your ideal week. I was talking with one of my clients about this recently and she found this so simple and brilliant she was recalling how she was asking her father (who recently retired and is possibly starting to suffer with depression) to complete the same task.

So here you take a piece of paper and divide it into 7 columns, one for each day of the week. You can go all out with this and use coloured pens or highlighters or just a straightforward ballpoint pen. You might want to start by jotting down some ideas on a separate piece of paper and brain-dumping your ideal week. What's really important here is that you don't consider the barriers to what you want to achieve. Don't second guess what people might say or think, just put it all down on paper. There may be things that you are not able to achieve straight away but that doesn't mean you shouldn't put them down anyway.

What's great about this exercise is that once you get going, what you think you want and what you actually want are always the same thing. We also get to play-out some of our family stories and realise that often we have ideas about what we 'want' based on things we have heard or seen over the years which we think are right or desirable but actually, when it comes down to it, are not. When we give ourselves the freedom to really expose our desires we give ourselves the opportunity to achieve them.

That is the most important thing.

So you will be writing down your perfect week and this will include you in regards to all of your roles, mummy, wife, employee or boss-of-me and most importantly you as You!

Then take a moment to really look at it and digest it. How does it look? Is it right first time or does it need a few amendments? How close to it are you now? What needs to change in order to get closer to it? You may be closer than you think which is amazing and that in itself is the beauty of the exercise. Sometime we don't realise what we have until we see it spelt out in black and white (or technicolour) in front of us.

For others though, it may mean assessing the situation and working out what they need to do to get closer to it. What changes do you need to make and whose help do you need in order to accommodate this? This may mean that you need to be resourceful in who you are asking help from. For some it may mean asking their partner, or ex-partner, if there are children involved, family members, friends and school friends/parents. Or it might mean speaking with your boss about your working hours or thinking creatively how to fit things in.

It will also likely mean working out how you are wasting time at the moment or having a view on what you need to stop doing in order to make the changes you want. What kind of things, big or small can you drop, move or delegate? How many hours in your week are spent doing things that are either not that important or could be done by someone else? How much time do you waste being idle? Don't get me wrong, everyone needs downtime. I don't mean you need to be a robot or Duracell bunny, but equally there may be points in the day where you are killing empty time and this could be better used doing something more meaningful to you.

If you have done the first part of this exercise this may be a lot easier to work out as you will have evidence of your days and weeks. However, if you haven't then some of this will be guess work.

The whole point of this chapter is to help you spend your time feeling happy and in control of your life. There are some aspects of our life where we don't have as much control as we might like. We have to work to pay our bills, the children have to go to school and we might have certain commitments or duties that we are, for now, bound to but in the main we are the ones who have control of what we do and don't do. Everything that we do, have and are, with only a few exceptions, is down to us either creating or allowing it. So be honest with yourself about what you are allowing into your life.

Ask yourself, is this as good as it gets? Am I happy to be doing this for the next year or five? What do you need to change or tweak in order to be living your best life? Be accountable for your life. Don't be the person that moans and groans and yet is not willing to do anything about it, because that's dull.

Moaning is depressing. It's a negative energy that drains your soul and taints the souls of everyone around you. Don't be that person!

If something isn't right, fix it. You have the power to change it. If you are ill you either go to the chemist or the doctor. If something is wrong with the car you take it to the garage. If something at home is broken and irreparable you throw it out and yet so often our most precious asset, our self, we treat really badly and compromise on so many things.

Know what you want and be the person who changes it.

8. PERSONAL DEVELOPMENT AND GOALS

What do you want in your life that you have either not managed to achieve yet or that you think is so far-out that it would never be possible? There are so many things that we can have these days and I firmly and genuinely believe that we can have pretty much anything we want, if we are willing to believe we can have it and deserve it and set our minds to go get it no matter what.

Now I'm not talking about marrying a billionaire nor having a house in the Caribbean, although, to be fair, neither of those are impossible either if you actually set your mind to it.

What I'm talking about is what you want for yourself, and maybe your family, in the year or few years ahead. So what do I mean by this? When I break this down with my clients, and I have done this for myself many times too, it's often quite surprising to discover what it is we actually want. Often, but not always, what the overwhelming majority of women want is time and financial freedom. We can present this in many different ways but ultimately what we want is time to spend with our family, do nice things and to have the money to achieve it. That's actually it, quite plain and simple.

Now, don't get me wrong, that is of course a huge sweeping statement. Within that also there are dreams of changes of careers, bigger homes, nicer cars, education and learning, travel and being a size 10 or 12, and of course all these things are perfectly achievable if you really want them to be.

I think one of the biggest difficulties we may have, (and I am speaking to women, for women, because that is the majority of my client base and friendship/network circle, but like everything in this book, it can apply to men too) is not being able to dream big. Not being able to prioritise our own wishes and feelings above those of our loved ones. Why is that? At what point did we become so programmed and hard wired that we lost the ability to follow our dreams.

When you were a young child what did you dream? What did you role play and what did you think life had in store for you? I never dreamed of being a princess or marrying Prince Charming, but I did have dreams of having a lovely house and a wonderful family and being something wonderful like a 'child psychologist' or someone who helped people.

Well, 35 years on and Ta Da! Wow! I mean, YES! I have it, but there was a time (and I mean a long time, many years) that just being able to pay the mortgage and have food in the cupboard and heat in the pipes was as good as it got. Anything over and above that was a bonus.

There comes a time for many of us where the childhood dreams and expectation of life somehow fade away and we get caught up in the routine and humdrum.

I can remember watching Carol Dweck talking about this in a TedEx talk once and referring to how children lose their appetite for learning and some fall into the cycle of a fixed mindset where they are unable to get beyond the idea of 'not achieved YET' and instead see failure.

This really resonated with me and I think this is so true of many women today.

This in combination with being raised as nurturers and empaths, which obviously we do naturally because we are innately gifted at both, means we can all too easily fall into the rut of providing care for our family and loved ones and negate our own position because quite frankly, it's too exhausting to do anything else.

As I have said previously, we do tend to be the ones that have to spin the plates of career and family because in the main, it's just how it is. Many women put their careers on hold in order to be able to look after their family and even if their career has not been halted in any way, are more likely to be the ones to have a day off work if their child is ill, be the arranger of childcare, run the household etc.

But what about the big dreams? Does it mean that just because that's how it's always been nothing need ever change? Can you dare to dream big and if not, why not? What is it that actually stands in your way of even saying your big dream out loud, or even better, writing it down?

There is something very cementing about writing stuff down. We can keep stuff in our head all day long but the moment it is written down it somehow becomes more real. In fact, an essential part of goal setting is writing it down and committing to it. Most mindset coaches will advise you to write out your goals every single day because the more you write them down the greater the chance there is of them coming true, but we'll come onto that a bit later.

For now I want to encourage you to think big. What is it you actually want? The best way to think about this might be to consider what you would wish for if you could wish for anything in the world (barring things like world peace and an end to pain and suffering, although that probably would be my one wish if that were in my control)

What I'm saying is if you could change one thing about your life, what would it be? Do this now. Sit for a moment and take as long as you need. Have a pen and paper handy and write it down. In fact, write down as many wishes as you like and then see if you can squeeze out a couple more. How crazy do you think you can go with these wishes? What kind of things do you think you can come up with? And then when you have done it, do you see a theme? Do any of your dreams and wishes link together?

What if, somehow, any of the wishes on your list were actually achievable? What would it mean to you to be able to put any of them into action? Start by rearranging your wishes into time scales so that you have some that you wish to be more immediate, some within the next weeks or months, then into the next year and then any that might be part of a longer, say five year, plan.

When you consider these wishes, do they seem ridiculous? Have any of them taken you by surprise and made you wonder where on earth they came from? Do you think that they are ridiculous or actually are you pleasantly surprised to see that a few of them are easily achievable?

I worked with a lady once who was so surprised by the list she created that she was able to action two of the points almost immediately. She hadn't realised how important it was to her to be able to work in a co-working space in the City of London and within three days she had located an office, arranged child care for her children, set up payment and hey-presto, was overlooking the Thames twice a week and all by the time our next session came around. It wasn't just about having a business that fitted around her family, you see. Initially, that was the dream, and that was her intention, but actually once that became her reality she realised that she needed more than that. She needed a level of human interaction that she wasn't getting from working at home and more than that she needed to feel more prestige. She didn't want to only work in her track-pants at home with her hair in a bun (although she absolutely loved doing that too) she also wanted to dress up and put her heels on, do her hair and makeup and get on a train to town and feel like she was 'someone' other than mother, homemaker, part time VA. Her wish, in that moment, was fulfilled.

So you see, it doesn't always need to be complicated. Sometimes it's about just being clear about what you want.

Let's take another example. What about training for a change of career, your dream career? How do you do that when you are already exhausted by life and don't have enough time or energy to see your friends for a night out, let alone anything else?

What do you consider the difference to be between

mindset and self-limiting beliefs? I'm going to go into more detail on this in a later chapter but for now let's explore what you think you are capable of and where those beliefs come from.

So what is a self-limiting belief? It is a perception or assumption that we have about ourselves that prevents us from stepping out of our comfort zone and keeps us stuck where we are. There may be many different reasons why we hold such beliefs but usually these will start in childhood and will have been shaped and formed over the years by our experiences which, though not exclusively, will have been negative and therefore reinforce the stories we hold about ourselves.

Self-limiting beliefs are not the same as (poor) self-esteem, although they can certainly inform and affect each other. Belief in your own ability to achieve certain things may not be a direct result of your self-esteem, although if you constantly limit your growth and thoughts of development this could well be indicative of a low opinion of yourself to do well/better.

Self-limiting beliefs could simply be thinking that you are too old to try something new, that you don't have the time to learn a new skill or that you can't break or form a habit because you have tried it before and it didn't work. These examples have little to do with low confidence or self-esteem and more to do with creating barriers for yourself that are simply untrue or unnecessary.

If we consider a child who didn't do that well at school for reasons that were not about their actual capability but more to do with their home environment, that child may well grow-up with the belief that they are not clever but stupid and never going to achieve much. Because of this they may well walk through their life never putting themselves forward for education, promotion, challenges in life, because fundamentally they do not believe in their ability to achieve. They may go on to get a reasonably good job and do very well in that position. They may learn over time that they are in fact able to do well and achieve, but deep-down they still consider themselves to be not clever enough to go to the next level. Their self-limiting beliefs may be that they don't deserve to be where they are now and it's only because no-one better has come along that they are still in their job, or that their personality has got them to where they are now but actually one day they'll be found out as a fraud and fired for gross-incompetence or misleading others into believing in them – classic Imposter Syndrome, which affects far more people that you might realise. The tricky thing about such beliefs is that they are incredibly difficult to undo or re-learn.

A belief is simply a feeling of certainty about what something means. The reason it can feel so certain is because it's a story we have been telling ourselves throughout our lives, unconsciously looking for proof that it's true. We find plenty of evidence because that's what we are looking for and the more we find, the more certain we feel. This means we can either create more potential or more limitation depending on what the belief actually is.

So that is why when we are thinking about goals and what we want to achieve we must not stop to think 'practical'. When we get caught up considering why it's not possible, the financial implications, the time it will take, the 'what will people think of me' we lose the passion to just think big. What about if you could just free-style your goals and not limit them based on your value of yourself or hurdles in the way? Because this is ultimately about what you think you deserve. So often I talk to my clients about self-worth and what they really feel they deserve in life, which could be love, relationships, money, career, anything they want.

I've talked about this earlier in the book but I'm going to say it again because if there's anything I want you to take away from this book, this is it!

The only thing that truly stands in the way of you and your dreams is you! If you want something badly enough you can have it! The problem is very rarely about time or money but invariably about how you feel about yourself and whether or not you think you are good enough to have your dream.

You can goal set, manifest, meditate and visualise but if that little voice in your ear is telling you that you are a dreamer, spoilt, ridiculous or greedy then you won't achieve it. Or you will achieve it but then probably won't be able to keep hold of it.

Self-sabotage around things that make you happy is a real thing. Dreaming of having true love, the lasting kind, if you have grown up feeling invisible, unworthy of love or mistreated as a child, is going to be tricky not because you don't deserve it but because you don't feel you deserve it. So many of my clients have had true love, but have tested it so much, pushing, prodding and poking it that it ended up leaving them because they didn't believe they were worthy of having it and reinforced that to themselves by losing it.

It's the same with financial goals. If you believe that your net worth is £30,000, you'll never get to £60,000 no matter how hard you try because your self-belief is that no-one will ever pay you more than that and you'd have to do something crazy to achieve it.

When I first put my prices up to £90 an hour while I was still counselling clients, I felt physically sick. It was only through the amazing work of my own coach that I had the courage to do it. I was amazed when people started paying me that amount. I thought I had to be someone so much better than 'me' to be charging that rate. Even though my education, training and experience is vast and far exceeds some of my peers, I just couldn't believe that was my hourly rate. When my coach told me that one day I'd be doubling that and put it into a coaching package where I'd be changing the lives of others, but more importantly building a life for myself and my family that would make my dreams come true, I laughed but also felt strangely excited. She had total faith in me and I was by this time also starting to have faith in myself too. I remember the day I called her after I had signed up my second coaching client at that higher rate. It had taken some mega-mindset work to get there and if I'm honest, I needed to get the second one on-board to prove to myself the first one wasn't a fluke.

Investing in your mindset is the most important thing you can do in order to achieve your goals. Investing the money on my first coach was exactly that. It was an investment. I learned to understand my blocks, my hurdles to reaching my goals. I sent a very clear message to myself that I was not only worth the financial investment (even though it made me feel sick at the time), but also that I wasn't above my own story and that we all have blocks to our growth, no matter how enlightened we think we are.

Every time we grow and we reach a new level we reach new blocks. None of us is immune to that. The power comes from being aware of our self-limiting beliefs and understanding that they are just that. We all have the power to achieve our goals if we set our mind to them and believe in ourselves enough to achieve them.

9. MINDSET

So let's have a think about mindset. Most of you have probably come across the idea of this although it may mean different things to each of you. Some of you may see it as a casual term meaning generally whether or not you are a positive go-getter or somebody whose cup is always half empty and generally quite down on life. Throughout this book everything, in one way or another, has come down to mindset and that is because in the end I firmly believe everything does.

Let's look at it in a few different ways. Carol Dweck's original work and research on mindset categorised individuals into two sets: fixed and growth mindset. She studied and researched students in education and found there were some who did not think that they were able to achieve good results and were stuck in their belief of not being able to do better (fixed) and others who, although may not have achieved good results first time around, considered this as not achieved 'yet' and an opportunity to do better (growth).

This is hugely significant and in many ways the whole premise of what mindset actually means. We all know by now that our early experiences form part of our adult personalities and characteristics and whether or not we go through life with high or low confidence and self-esteem. Please note at this stage I am not talking about whether we go through life confident and achieving because I don't believe that the two are intrinsically linked, although obviously, they may correlate. You can have those that don't necessarily 'achieve' but had great confidence, and those achieve greatly but massively lack confidence, but let's just stick to mindset for now.

To some of you, mindset might be something that is a positive or negative. We all hear a lot about having a positive mindset or a positive mental attitude and for those who have such mindset, a growth mindset, nothing is ever really off-limits, unachievable or final. Those with this mindset will see failure as an opportunity for learning and growth. You see, those of us who seek perpetual learning in every opportunity, good and bad, will always be looking for the golden nugget because there is always a golden nugget if you have the right mindset!

Conversely, those who feel either they are not good enough to do better or not equipped with enough time or money to take an opportunity never will, or will find it very hard. They may feel life has either held them back, pushed them down or they have taken every knockback and hurdle as a reason or excuse to feel that the world is against them. It is really very simple because the ability to bounce back after every knock and bump in the road takes courage. It takes guts, grit and determination, but more than that bouncing back is the essential ingredient of growth. It takes the ability to self-reflect. It requires you to be able to examine and to be honest with yourself in determining both your strengths and your flaws. You are required to take every opportunity, good and bad, as an opportunity to learn, develop and grow. Sounds simple? Well believe me, it is not! There is nothing remotely simple about trying to see an opportunity to learn and grow at the times when it hurts the most. Or maybe it's something else? Maybe it's about considering which path to take. We are often presented with junctions in our life and sometimes knowing which decision to make, which path to choose, can be just as challenging as anything else.

Ultimately having a mindset which allows you to be constantly moving forward, constantly looking for ways to improve yourself or your life situation can also be quite exhausting. Maybe there is reason to examine your need to never sit still. Do you always want more, never feeling satisfied with what you have? It's an interesting conundrum. How do we decide when enough is enough, or is it never really enough? Do we always want more because we can and so we should or should we consider that if our bucket is never full it is possibly because there is a hole in it in which case we need to address that issue and fix it? That is the great thing about mindset. It can be your greatest friend or your biggest foe and really it's just down to you to decide whether or not your glass is half full or half empty. Either way though, we all have the ability to refill if we choose to do so, regardless of our situation or environment.

I was talking with a friend recently about a new promotion that she had achieved. The position was two levels above her previous role and so she was now managing her former manager. She contemplated whether she was good enough for this position, even though she had begun to realise that her manager actually wasn't all that great. However, she still felt like a little fish in a big pond. I put it to her that there are thousands of people in higher management roles, who quite frankly should never have got the job in the first place but worked their way up because in their mind they are winners, not questioning their ability, oozing confidence. It is that very confidence that got them where they are. They don't question their ability even though they really should. At some point they set their minds on getting the job and then they just kept going until they got it.

Conversely, there are great people stuck in the job or position they are in simply because they don't have the confidence to go forward and try something new or put themselves in a position where they might have to fail a few times in order to get where they want to be. This is such a terrible shame because they would probably do a far better job than the people they are possibly looking up to and yet their mindset doesn't allow them to have faith in themselves or their ability to learn from their falls and keep getting up. The biggest achievers in life, truly, are the ones who always get back up, no matter how hard they fall. They dust themselves off, learn, adapt, try again, and again, until they succeed.

So how do you relate to this? Where are you on the scale? Are you always inching forwards, step-by-step, gradually or do you dive-in and throw yourself at life? Maybe you find comfort in your excuses, your safe spot, your comfort zone? You consider maybe now isn't the right time, or money is not your friend, or you'll think about it when things have settled down a bit, the kids are older, or you have more time on your hands? These are all viable excuses to someone who believes that other people are just lucky, handed opportunities on a plate. They don't know the hardship that 'I' have to go through, 'my' life isn't that straightforward.

When I worked with Sally, she had got herself into quite a rut, emotionally speaking. She had been married for several years and I think was really quite bored. She had a lovely husband and two lovely children but she felt very stuck. She had everything that she had ever wanted: a beautiful family, a lovely home, no financial concerns, and yet she was miserable. Not ungrateful, just miserable. She was desperate for something but she didn't know what.

After a considerable amount of work and soul-searching she realised that the issue wasn't her marriage or her family but was actually unresolved issues in herself. We often consider that the grass is greener on the other side and yet the reality is often anything but. Seeing life through either rose tinted lenses or just out of focus ones doesn't give us a true understanding or perspective of the reality. I presented Sally with several opportunities after we had done a lot of work around her goals, blocks and of course, mindset. I suggested to her that she had some space and that she took some time to really consider what it was she wanted. Did she really want to separate from her husband and break up her family unit (a thought that terrified her and excited her in equal measures) or did she need to do something else? She took herself off for a weekend, pretty much in isolation, to a little cottage down by the coast. There, in addition to having time to herself and reflecting on life's most important questions, she also did a lot of her favourite hobby which was drawing and painting; something that she *loved doing but often lacked the time to do. She also had a few glasses of wine, had time to have a hot bath, listen to some podcasts and essentially to nurture her soul. She promptly realised that the issue wasn't her marriage or her family, but that she had, as is the case with so many of my clients, been so busy looking after everyone else she had totally fallen short of looking after herself. She realised that her sense of lacking was about her own fulfilment. It seems so easy to say that simply one weekend away had solved all her problems and of course that wasn't the case. However, it was enough time for her to be able to really contemplate what was missing for her and to discover that it was a piece of herself; a part of her which had been so neglected she had pretty much forgotten that it had existed.*

We had had many sessions where we had spoken about her childhood, emotions and feelings about her mother, various other issues that had impacted on her emotional vulnerability as well as well-being and so the weekend away to immerse herself in love and self-care was the final cherry on the cake, essential and so completely pivotal for her. She went back home not only rested but with a completely new appreciation for her family. The things which she felt were the real issue simply were not. The children bickering, the messy house, the mundane job were just a part of life which most people have, are most likely annoyed by, but not to the extent of wanting to make a life-changing decision. Once she realised that the grass absolutely would not have been greener on the other side but would have been quite toxic for her and her family, she realised the things she needed to do in order to look after herself and feed her soul. She made more time for self-care, more time for exercise, art, time with friends and promptly started applying for new jobs. You see, her family situation was merely a reflection of how she was feeling about herself. Her family loved and adored her and of course she absolutely adored them too, but because she wasn't clear on what she needed to keep herself happy she was looking at her family situation through blurred lenses.

We all have blurred lenses at times and sometimes all we need to do is just take them off to be able to see things clearly. Sometimes it really is about perspective and how we interpret and value our position. So what situation in your life are you looking at with blurred lenses? What area of your life gives you frustration? Ask yourself this: is this a situation that needs to change or is it something that needs to be approached differently? If you need to approach it differently, in your wildest craziest thoughts, what would you do in order to see a good enough improvement for you, either immediately or in the near future? Sometimes there are things in life that we can change but if we can't change the problem then maybe we need to change our attitude to the problem.

We all have the ability to go through life feeling there are certain areas that we can't control. Whether that is our health, relationships or our ability to learn from our experiences the fact of the matter is that we all have the ability to enact free choice. We are all able to see the glass either half full or half empty. To recite a meme I once saw on Facebook, it doesn't matter if the glass is half full or half empty all you need to do is fill it up. You can choose to be defined by your past and your limited self-beliefs or you can choose to make a change today. I genuinely believe there is nothing that we don't have control over. Changes may not happen overnight, that is for sure. Some changes, big changes, take time to implement but one small step every day can make an enormous difference over time and that is the point I'm trying to make. If you start something today and make a commitment to that change, then the outcome can only be different. Our path changes by the decisions we make every day. Every tiny decision we make impacts our journey. So what are the blocks you put in your way? What are the stories you tell yourself or repeatedly replay in your mind that you have heard? I challenge you to give this deep consideration. What small changes can you make today that in a year's time you'll look back on and thank yourself for?

10. SELF CARE

How do you look after yourself? What do you think about when you hear the words self-care? Is it a luxury for people who have more time and money than you do or is it an absolute necessity that is non-negotiable for you? Self-care can of course cover a whole array of things from painting your nails, having time out to get lost in a good book, daily exercise or a weekend retreat. It doesn't really matter how you qualify it, what's important is that you do it.

Too easily we can get so carried away with the hamster wheel of life that looking after and nurturing ourselves can be forgotten. Maybe you consider that you put so much time and energy into looking after everyone else it would be nice for someone to look after you for a change. The problem with that is that being shown appreciation for what you do for your family, isn't self-care but just the flip-side of caring for others. Sitting down and having a quiet five minutes while your husband takes the girls out for a bike ride or to their swimming lesson isn't self-care, that's just balance and if you're anything like me you'll be either working or catching up on house chores in that time anyway.

I think about self-care as being more about mindset than anything else. I believe it ultimately comes down to how much you value yourself and what you are willing to give yourself as a reward for being you. Do you consider that getting your nails done every couple of weeks is self-care? I personally don't but I completely understand why others do. For me, self-care is my exercise routine. It's about getting up early, before the children wake up and spending an hour working on my mind and body. Others might not see that as self-care but as torture. Or they may have the same view as I do about nails, that it's nice to have it done but it's more about maintaining an image rather than looking after yourself.

I suppose for me the ultimate self-care (in addition to exercise) is seeing my friends. It doesn't matter if this is with my children or without them. Just being able to be completely at ease, relaxing and having fun, usually with a couple of glasses of wine and lots of laughter.

When I get to a point in my head where I need *friendapy* (I totally just made that up) then that's it. My friends are my therapy and they can turn a bad day or week completely around within a couple of hours. Being able to be with 'my people' and be totally at ease and relaxed is the best therapy for me. Admittedly it doesn't happen very often, or I should say, not as often as it could. I hesitate here slightly for a couple of reasons. I am very lucky in that I have never found being around my children hard work. I rarely (I mean really rarely) tire of them so much that I need a break from them. I love the school holidays and always feel a bit crushed when they have to go back to school. They light my soul and being with them makes my heart sing.

Most of my friends have children too and so getting together with my friends, wherever that may be, feels absolutely fine to me. Of course a night out with the girls is something different and being able to chat uninterrupted, have a few drinks and enjoy a nice meal without having to worry about what you're saying is so much fun. But equally, I can just as much enjoy watching the children play in the park or on the beach. It doesn't matter what you do, as long as it is right for you.

If for you self-care is about having a night off from family life, or even a weekend away from it with your friends or partner, that is absolutely fine. It may be that you love having a hot bath listening to music or you may consider self-care a weekly session to see a counsellor or coach, it really is whatever you need it to be. It should enrich you, enhance and energise you. The benefits of this are mainly to yourself but will also have a huge impact on all of your relationships too. Creating space for yourself makes you a better person, not in terms of being virtuous or righteous but in terms of resetting the balance.

Make sure you have time with people that make you feel at ease and relaxed without needing to be on-guard or subdued. This also means protecting your relationship and carving out time to be with your partner which can often be very difficult, especially when children and work take up most of your time and energy. Ensuring that you have quality time with your partner is essential in maintaining a strong and healthy relationship. This could mean having regular date nights (however frequently you decide is important to you both), making time for intimacy, not just in terms of sex (though that is important) but also in terms of connecting emotionally. We've already spoken about the importance of communication and so we understand by now why we need to work hard at keeping all channels open, metaphorically and physically. But this is more about creating the space and energy that energises you both as a couple and keeps you in touch with your shared goals and values.

Self-care ultimately is about looking after and prioritising yourself.

Let's consider a few more examples of self-care that might not necessarily spring to mind.

What about that back-ache you've had for the last few weeks? The blood tests you feel you need to get done as you're always tired, speaking with a professional around unresolved family issues or grief, going to the chiropodist because the corns on your feet are causing you pain when you walk?

Here's a great one: learning to say NO! Wow! This one is SO important and probably one of the hardest to implement for so many women! How many times have you been asked to do something and inside your head you screamed 'no' but the words 'sure, no problem' come out of your mouth instead? This could be going out to do something when all you want to do is chill out on the sofa in your Pjs or going to a work social, or running an errand for someone or just simply agreeing to do something you don't want to do simply to avoid an argument or another episode of conflict. This happens to us women all the time. Why? Because we are inherently people-pleasers who mostly (not in all cases obviously) find it easier to roll our sleeves up and get on with it rather than just say no. Born nurturers, we find it easier to do right by others rather than doing right by ourselves.

Learning to say no when we need to is probably one of the most effective ways to practice self-care there is. It's not about being stubborn and selfish, it's about valuing yourself enough to know where your limit is and understanding your boundaries. Being able to value yourself is ultimately what this entire chapter (and book) is about. We may often be fearful about what others may think about us if we say no, that they might judge us unfairly, hold resentment towards us or talk badly about us and yet even though I have over the years been at times paralysed by being a people-pleaser I have always had the utmost admiration for others who are able to simply say 'no' to a request that doesn't fit their time or energy. I don't think ill of them (well maybe occasionally I might do), but in the main I envy their ability to simply protect themselves enough to say no without worrying about the consequences. Creating and maintaining good personal boundaries is empowering to yourself but also eliminates any future feelings of resentment that might occur towards the person who is asking you.

What about diet and sleep? Do you consider these to be examples of self-care? Everyone has to eat and sleep, right? I am not the fun police by any stretch of the imagination but I have always considered these to be absolutely essential to maintaining good emotional and physical well-being. Understanding the impact of a healthy balanced diet is just so important. Being aware of the food and drink we put into our body is one of the best ways we can look after ourselves. Eating stuff that is either junk or that we know doesn't agree with us, even if we love it, is simply not valuing ourselves and our bodies. Going out and having a night off to eat a pizza or drink wine or gin is probably not going to do us any harm but repeating patterns of putting either excess or toxic substances, whatever they may be, into our body is just not setting the right environment to be able to prioritise what our body wants and needs.

Equally, not getting enough sleep because we are staying up too late, spending too much time on our screens, or, as has been the case with me, drinking too much wine or Prosecco knowing that it is going to significantly affect my sleep is just not cool even if it is great fun at the time (remember, I have never put myself on a pedestal and I, like you, am equally flawed).

Ensuring a good healthy diet, limiting your alcohol consumption, doing regular exercise and ensuring you are getting enough sleep, is, without doubt, an excellent example of valuing and caring for yourself.

Who will look after you if you can't look after yourself? Yes of course we may have loved ones who care for us, a partner to cook for us, friends to make us laugh, family to support us, but that's not the same as being able to look after yourself, to be able to understand the real story from within, not just what is shown on the outside. None of us is able to keep going all of the time without stepping off the hamster wheel and taking a break.

Being kind to yourself helps you to be the best version of you. Be kind to yourself.

11. AND SO TO SUMMARISE

I feel as if, in many respects, this book has been just the tip of the iceberg of what I want to deliver to you. Although it has covered several topics the main theme of it was (I hope) a pretty simple message. The most important thing I hope you have received is that the only person in charge of your well-being is you. You are your own best friend and your own worst enemy.

Being able to understand not only who we are but why we are is the most valuable bit of insight we can give ourselves. Ultimately, everything, I believe, comes down to how much we value ourselves and what we are willing to receive for ourselves.

We all get where we are for a hundred, million different reasons, decisions and outcomes. All our journeys are beautifully unique and yet so many of these stories are shared, with similar outcomes: that we can often end up feeling at the bottom of the pile, caring so well for everyone else and neglecting to care for ourselves or maybe managing to do it sometimes, but not consistently and not effectively. We know what we want but for some reason we're just not very good at doing it. We have taken on board the stories we heard when we were growing up and turned them into our truths, but so often those stories are wrong. So often the people who taught us those stories have themselves been told stories which were also wrong and these messages get received and repeated all down the line creating their own little narrative as they go.

Don't get me wrong, it's not all doom and gloom. Far from it in fact. Many of those stories can be equally wonderful. My professional background has given me a particular slice of reality which means that the ladies and couples that I help have themselves taken on their own truths, many of which weren't theirs to start with but have hindered them in some way or another. The work we do together rewrites those stories and that is why I am so blessed to have the job that I do.

None of us is perfect. Not me, not you and not her over there. And that is absolutely fine. We were not put here to be perfect but to learn and hopefully to improve ourselves, gradually, one day at a time.

If you believe that you are a good person and that you deserve good things, they will happen to you. You won't actually need to work that hard for it, it will naturally just happen. Too often we put obstacles in our own way. We might use excuses such as time, money or commitments but actually, most of the time that is simply not the case. When we set our minds to something, no matter how big or significant, if we believe we can have it and deserve it, I genuinely think we can.

And so all that I ask of you now is to be honest

with yourself about what you want. What do you need in order to create the future you want for yourself and what do you need to change? If you had the power to make one thing happen, one big change in your life, no questions or limitations, what would it be? Sometimes people go crazy with this question but most of the time it comes down to some sort of freedom. Whether that is time freedom, financial freedom or relationship freedom, that's usually where it's at.

So if that is the case for you, what is holding you back? What stories are you telling yourself that prevent you from living your best life? If you honestly feel that you can't go after your dreams because there is some sort of limitation holding you back I ask you to sit and consider those options and outcomes.

We all have limitations, let's not be unrealistic. Our big bold dream might not happen tomorrow. It might not even happen next year but with the right frame of mind and the right dose of self-worth and motivation everyone can create the life they want whether that's owning a flower shop, buying a five bedroom house in Spain or doing a PhD. Absolutely nothing is off limits.

I want you to Be Happy in Life and Love! And the best way to achieve that is by being kind to yourself, being compassionate to yourself and giving yourself a big shove in the right direction.

One small step, no matter how insignificant, each day, will in time get you to exactly where you need to be.

12. REFLECTIONS ON LOCKDOWN 2020

Since starting this book, something crazy happened that affected every corner of the world. You'll know it and you will have been affected by it, because we all were, without exception.

During the process of the Covid-19 lockdown, something very incredible happened. As well as the apocalyptic silence that spread across our world, every emotion possible was felt and for me, it felt like I transitioned through something really quite profound.

First of all, I need to acknowledge that I have not been affected by the virus. My family, friends and loved ones remain healthy and well and I am incredibly grateful for that. I have lost no-one, and while I know a few people personally who have been ill, none have been significantly (life-threateningly) ill. I am grateful for that and I am so sorry for those that have been less fortunate.

I know also that people have lost their jobs, have had financial struggles, been isolated and alone, been locked down in abusive or toxic relationships and have had to endure weeks of pain and suffering. I have not and I am very grateful for that.

In fact, I have had many conversations where I have felt guilty or ashamed telling people how much I have loved lockdown and what a blessing it has been for both me and my family. It feels uncomfortable when so many others have suffered, it has been an incredible experience which I doubt I will ever get again. My family and my business have thrived and although that comes down to a lot of hard work and effort, I can't help but feel like the luckiest girl in the world.

In the early part of lockdown, it all felt very

uncertain. We were all apprehensive of what was going to happen. The news coverage was both terrifying and sensationalist and visions of this *plague* spreading over the world was what we were all led to imagine what was in progress. It was scary, without a doubt. We all watch as the entire world literally ground to a halt. You couldn't make it up and if it was a movie, you'd never believe it. Cars stopped, shops shut, parks closed. Supermarket shelves became bare and the greed of some left others without for weeks.

In our little bubble at home though, we were ok. The calls for both Dave and I were coming in thick and fast and although we were cautious about how this period would affect our businesses, we didn't really have time to stop and think about it.

We isolated with our next door neighbours as we share our garden together, (having four girls between us of similar ages) and because of that, I was able to work, pretty much continuously, knowing the girls were not only safe and looked after but also having the time of their life. Was I riddled with guilt that I wasn't spending more time with them? Yes, absolutely. But actually, they were mostly too busy having fun to notice and when I wasn't working, I was definitely present and so I feel, all in all, it wasn't so bad. You see, I had a vision that I was very clear about and I felt like it was an opportunity to really grab with both hands. Having four adults in the combined home, looking after four children, meant that I could really dive into my business. Afterall, I am a relationship coach and I had a hunch that my services would be needed... which they were.

Interestingly, something happened to some of my clients that I hadn't anticipated. I had been worried how those with anxiety would manage lockdown and whether or not they would spiral out of control with fear and worry. I worried too for my husband Dave who also suffers from it and what affect this would have on us as a family.

Then I spoke with a few people and realized that lockdown was providing them with a sense of relief that was both calming and empowering. There was no need to 'perform' for the outside world but instead they were allowed to be their perfect self, secure in their bubble of home, without having to step out into the noise of the world because, there was no noise. This incredible effect of being still was so incredible that it felt quite lifechanging. I wonder for those affected what that sense of relief must have felt like. As if someone who has live with chronic pain were able to wake up pain free and live a 'normal' life without having to anticipate or second guess every move they make.

It was so lovely to see Dave without anxiety for a decent period of time, even if only for a few short weeks. He was no doubt busy with work, but he was relaxed and he appeared to be in control of his emotions. That's the problem with anxiety. The person suffering has no control over what they are feeling or when it's going to take them. Observing a loved one who lives with it can be heartbreaking. It can also be frustrating and draining as you have to pick up the pieces that are left behind, as the anxiety creates a vicious cycle of exhaustion which takes the person off to bed at all different times of the day in order to recover.

But I digress. The start of 2020 was no doubt a time for reflection for everyone. The things that we took for granted were promptly taken away from us and what we had left we were left to savor. My family, like many others, really had time to just *be,* without any external forces telling us how it needed to be. Yes there was schoolwork that needed to be done, but even that was very loosely attempted. Being that the girls are only 7 and 4 at the time of writing this, I really wasn't worried that their life choices were going to be seriously compromised by having three months off school. They did some, and Amélie loved doing some word and maths games online, but really and truthfully, I wasn't that bothered. And let me be honest, the amount of hours I was working, there was no way I was going to be spending my precious time with them doing homework.

Instead they spent hours playing in the garden; Dave had the incredible foresight to know exactly what was coming in February and had managed to buy an incredible two-story playhouse with swings and slide off Facebook marketplace which he promptly put up in the garden the weekend before school shut down. Commonly referred to as 'Corona Castle', they girls have relished every minute of their time in it.

I taught my youngest how to ride a bike and an overwhelming sense of gratitude enveloped me like never before. How did I get to be this lucky? How did I manage to get a family so beautiful and so together? How did I manage to grow a business that I not only love, but that helps people through such difficult times? How did I manage to finish a book while all of this was going on?

I feel like this chapter is a bit oily. That is not my intention. I have worked very hard on myself and on my mindset in recent years and lockdown has been a very unique period of time for us all. I have no doubt that some of the things I have learnt are not to everyone's tase or satisfaction. That is absolutely fine.

I have learned to be humble and live in gratitude for everything I have and everything I have achieved. It has not been an easy path. In fact, at times it has nearly killed me. I don't know how I would have managed this period a few years ago. In fact, Dave and I were talking over dinner a couple of nights ago and he said something that made me gasp and smile in a way that only he can. He said 'I don't think I would have been able to cope spending this amount of time with you all (me and the girls) before, but I am pleased that we have and it's been quite nice'. Thanks Dave! I know exactly what he means though.

We have had space to grow with each other and share our time and thoughts together. Having shared goals and values makes this so much easier. Not goals in terms of monetary or lifestyle but in terms of how we want to raise our family and what is important to us both.

Running a business like mine feeds my soul. There is no doubt about that. Through the work that I do with my clients (and of course the studying I have done to get here), I am without doubt, a better person. Not a *better* person, I mean a better version of me. That's all I ever strive for really. Just to be the best version of me. The best mummy, the best wife, the best friend and the best coach. Yes, I have big dreams too. I make no apology for that. I want to go big. But that's not what this is about. In my calm and reflective state, I know that having big bold dreams are nothing if you don't have your loved ones to share it with.

The struggle is real. And we all do it in our own way. Ultimately, we are all just trying to do our best and get through each stage of our lives in the best way possible. It is not always easy. Sometimes its excruciating. But I really hope that this book provides some insight or support as to what to grab hold of and what to let go of.

When we live with peace and gratitude, everything feels different. We all have the ability to do that. We all have the ability to see the glass half empty or half full. And we all have the ability to fill that glass up whenever we want to.

Writing this book has been the most incredible experience for me I could ever have dreamt of. For years and years, I have wanted to write, but have always felt paralysed to do it. This book has literally written itself. It has been both effortless and empowering. I'm sure there will be others in the future but for now, this is where it ends.

I really hope that it has given you a nugget or two that will help you to make the changes in your life that you need.

Everyone has the right and ability to be Happy in Life and Love and all you need to do is give yourself permission to do it x

ABOUT THE AUTHOR

Pascale Lane is a Therapeutic Relationship and Life Coach, wife and mother of two. Her work is a unique combination of counselling and life coaching which enables her to support her clients therapeutically as well as helping them move forwards, towards their goals.

She works with individuals and couples struggling with relationship difficulties and helps them to identify the root cause in order to find a solution that provides long lasting change.

She does this with a Time-Limited package of work that provides her clients with both therapeutic support as well as accountability for their future.

Pascale's professional background combines 18 years social work experience working with vulnerable children and families, supporting both children, young people and families to create a safe and nurturing environment for...

During this time, she qualified as an attachment-based counsellor before qualifying with the national charity Relate as a relationship counsellor. She moved into Coaching after she realised that she was far more effective in combining all of her years of professional and lived experience and prefers to be more directive in her approach.

Pascale offers a unique combination of compassion, empathy and encouragement whilst keeping it real in her very relaxed, confident and friendly style.

She speaks readily and openly about her own experiences and because of this is considered approachable and relatable by her clients.

Pascale grew up in Sutton, South London where she currently lives with her husband Dave and their two daughters, Amélie and Jasmine. It is because of her children that she has designed her business to work around them and created a life that will support them in every aspect.

Pascale has always been a people's person and considers herself to have great sense of intuition and empathy. She has a strong sense of spirituality and is a follower of the Law of Attraction and is a manifesting Queen. She is also a practising Christian and raises her children, with her husband, in faith.

She is an exercise enthusiast, loves yoga and jogging and follows a vegan diet.

Work offered:

Pascale offers a 1-1 coaching program which she delivers via an online video platform enabling her to work with women, supporting them to increase the confidence and self-esteem by identifying blocks caused from historic or current relationship difficulties.

<u>Contact Information:</u>

E-mail: pascale@youfulfilled.com

Website: www.youfulfilled.co.uk

Printed in Poland
by Amazon Fulfillment
Poland Sp. z o.o., Wrocław

61565657R00110